Research Skills

How to Find It!

Circle Pines, Minnesota 55014-1796
800-328-2560
www.agsnet.com

Acknowledgments
Encyclopedia excerpts on pages 32 and 34 are reprinted with permission from *Compton's Encyclopedia*, © 2002 by Encyclopædia Britannica, Inc.

The encyclopedia excerpt on page 33 is reprinted from *Oxford American Children's Encyclopedia, 9 Vols.*, edited by Ann T. Keene, copyright © 2002 by Oxford University Press, Inc. Used by permission of Oxford University Press, Inc.

Publisher's Project Staff
Vice President, Product Development: Kathleen T. Williams, Ph.D., NCSP; Associate Director, Product Development: Teri Mathews; Assistant Editor: Sarah Brandel; Development Assistant: Bev Johnson; Creative Services Manager: Nancy Condon; Project Coordinator/Designer: Laura Henrichsen; Desktop Production Artist: Peggy Vlahos; Materials Management: Carol Nelson; Senior Marketing Manager: Brian Holl

Developed by Cynthia Woerner

Cover Image: background © Don Bishop/Getty Images

© 2004 AGS Publishing
4201 Woodland Road
Circle Pines, MN 55014-1796
800-328-2560 • www.agsnet.com

AGS Publishing is a trademark and trade name of American Guidance Service, Inc.

All rights reserved, including translation. No part of this publication may be reproduced or transmitted in any form or by any means without written permission from the publisher.

Printed in the United States of America

Product Number 92100
ISBN 0-7854-3663-4

A 0 9 8 7 6 5 4 3 2 1

CONTENTS

Introduction

When you first open this worktext, you might ask, "Why do I need to know this stuff?" The fact is, there is so much information that it can be hard to find just what you need. Why, you ask, do you need to know how to find information?

First, you will be writing papers for school. You will need to know how to find information for your papers. Perhaps for your history class you need to write about the American Revolution. There are thousands of books on the American Revolution! Which ones should you read? Where can you find them

Second, you might be surprised to know that you will need to find information in your daily life. Perhaps you want to know how to keep an aquarium. Some types of fish eat other types of fish. You would not want to put them in the same aquarium! Or you might want to repair your own car. Do you know how to change the oil, or why you need to change the oil?

Finally, you might just want to know something. What if someone told you that the century plant is a desert plant that grows in the southwestern United States. It lives from 25 to 75 years and only blooms once in its entire life. After it blooms, it dies. Are these facts? Is this information true? How could you find out?

Research Skills: How to Find It! teaches you step by step how and where to find information. Each lesson includes three parts. The first part is a class practice page. It tells you about the skills you will learn in the lesson. It also has practice questions that you and the rest of your class can work on together.

The second part is a group practice page. It has questions and exercises that you and a few other students can work on together. Working together can help you learn the skill.

The third part includes questions and exercises for you to do alone. This part of the lesson gives you practice so that you can master the new skill.

And you will have some fun along the way. Most of the lessons include a "Did You Know?" box. Each box includes a fact about the world. Perhaps that one little fact will lead you to discover even more information. Perhaps you will even start your own list of "Did You Know?" facts.

Whether you need information for writing a paper, fixing your bike, or making a cake, with practice and a little help from this book, you'll be an expert on how to find it.

LESSON 1 Order! Order!

WORDS TO KNOW

alphabetical order
the order of the letters of the alphabet, from A to Z

Class Practice

You use the alphabet every day. When you use a dictionary or a phone book, you are using the alphabet. The words in a dictionary and the names in a phone book are in alphabetical order. **Alphabetical order** means in the order of the alphabet, from A to Z.

If all the words start with different letters, they are arranged by the first letter of each word. If all the words start with the same letter, they are arranged by the second letter of each word: **dare, desk, dollar**. If all the words start with the same two letters, they are arranged by the third letter of each word: **ball, basket, batter**. Another rule to know about alphabetical order is "nothing before something." For example, **miss** comes before **misses,** and **brave** comes before **bravely**.

Rewrite the words in each group in alphabetical order.

1. sport ____________
spot ____________
spoon ____________

2. pattern ____________
pause ____________
patient ____________

3. mule ____________
mutter ____________
musket ____________
music ____________

4. snarl ____________
snap ____________
snake ____________
snapped ____________

5. honor ____________
honey ____________
hone ____________
hook ____________

6. expert ____________
expect ____________
experience ____________
expensive ____________

7. mystery ____________
messenger ____________
midnight ____________
myth ____________
middle ____________
mysterious ____________

DID YOU KNOW?

The word **alphabet** comes from the first two letters of the Greek alphabet, **alpha** and **beta**.

Group Practice

Rewrite the words in each group in alphabetical order.

1. jaw ____________
jar ____________
jam ____________
jail ____________

2. brick ____________
bracelet ____________
broom ____________
bread ____________

3. opinion ____________
opossum ____________
open ____________
opposite ____________

4. leather ____________
leaves ____________
league ____________
lean ____________

5. meal ____________
measure ____________
meadow ____________
meat ____________

6. fortunate ____________
forgive ____________
forehead ____________
forever ____________

7. knowledge ____________
know ____________
known ____________
knowing ____________

8. treating ____________
treaty ____________
treat ____________
treats ____________

9. starve ____________
stare ____________
startle ____________
star ____________

10. glitter ____________
cloud ____________
banner ____________
glisten ____________
clover ____________
spirit ____________
bandage ____________
glide ____________
spine ____________
banana ____________
band ____________
close ____________

On Your Own

Rewrite the words in each group in alphabetical order.

1. crab ____________
country ____________
cotton ____________
cricket ____________

2. nose ____________
northern ____________
nonsense ____________
noon ____________

3. accept ____________
accuse ____________
accent ____________
accident ____________
according ____________

4. explode ____________
explain ____________
explore ____________
explanation ____________

5. protest ____________
protection ____________
prove ____________
proudly ____________
protect ____________
proud ____________

6. husky ____________
hurt ____________
hunger ____________
hurricane ____________
hurry ____________
hungry ____________

7. handle ____________
praise ____________
weather ____________
weave ____________
hatch ____________
weary ____________
prairie ____________
handsome ____________

8. whittle ____________
warrior ____________
wound ____________
whip ____________
wharf ____________
whiskers ____________
worry ____________
world ____________
waddle ____________

LESSON 2 Give Me a Cue

WORDS TO KNOW

lexicon
a dictionary

cue
a signal or a hint

Class Practice

A dictionary, or **lexicon**, has three sections: a beginning (A–F), a middle (G–P), and an end (Q–Z). Many dictionaries have color-coded pages. Other dictionaries have thumb tabs with letters. These are **cues** to help you find the section you need. When you are looking up a word, it is easier and faster if you can open your dictionary to the correct section. The color-coded pages and thumb tabs are guides to help you.

Rewrite each word in the word list under the section where it is found in the dictionary.

WORD LIST					
thousand	rodeo	outdoor	whittle	split	hound
fact	music	journey	escape	detective	dare
equation	unit	allow	pattern	nonsense	zone

Beginning Section A–F Words	Middle Section G–P Words	End Section Q–Z Words
1. ______	**7.** ______	**13.** ______
2. ______	**8.** ______	**14.** ______
3. ______	**9.** ______	**15.** ______
4. ______	**10.** ______	**16.** ______
5. ______	**11.** ______	**17.** ______
6. ______	**12.** ______	**18.** ______

19. In which section of the dictionary would your last name appear?

______

20. In which section of the dictionary would the name of your school appear?

______

DID YOU KNOW?

Noah Webster was the first person to write an American dictionary. It was published in 1806. It was called *A Compendious Dictionary of the English Language.*

Group Practice

Rewrite each word in the word list under the section where it is found in the dictionary.

WORD LIST				
period	museum	written	example	opinion
definition	interrupt	follow	alphabet	collection
quill	setting	unusual	represent	glossary

Beginning Section A–F Words	Middle Section G–P Words	End Section Q–Z Words
1. ____________	**6.** ____________	**11.** ____________
2. ____________	**7.** ____________	**12.** ____________
3. ____________	**8.** ____________	**13.** ____________
4. ____________	**9.** ____________	**14.** ____________
5. ____________	**10.** ____________	**15.** ____________

16. List three more words that appear in the **beginning section** of the dictionary. ____________ ____________ ____________

17. List three more words that appear in the **middle section** of the dictionary. ____________ ____________ ____________

18. List three more words that appear in the **end section** of the dictionary. ____________ ____________ ____________

Write a complete sentence using each word.

19. cue ________________________________

____

20. lexicon ________________________________

____

On Your Own

Rewrite each word in the word list under the section where it is found in the dictionary.

WORD LIST				
hesitate	syllable	banner	department	ordinary
question	persuade	justice	finally	average
exactly	yesterday	result	professor	trust

Beginning Section A–F	Middle Section G–P	End Section Q–Z
1. ____________	**6.** ____________	**11.** ____________
2. ____________	**7.** ____________	**12.** ____________
3. ____________	**8.** ____________	**13.** ____________
4. ____________	**9.** ____________	**14.** ____________
5. ____________	**10.** ____________	**15.** ____________

16. List three more words that appear in the **beginning section** of the dictionary. ____________ ____________ ____________

17. List three more words that appear in the **middle section** of the dictionary. ____________ ____________ ____________

18. List three more words that appear in the **end section** of the dictionary. ____________ ____________ ____________

Read *Words to Know* on page 8. Fill in the correct word in each sentence.

19. The actor waited behind the curtain for his ____________ to go on stage.

20. Another word for **lexicon** is ____________.

LESSON 3 Guide the Way

WORDS TO KNOW

guide words
two words at the top of a page in a dictionary

definition
the meaning of a word

Class Practice

Once you find the right section of the dictionary, you need to find the right page. **Guide words** appear at the top of each page in a dictionary. These words are the first and last words defined on that page. They are there to guide you to the correct page when you are looking up the **definition** of a word.

Look up these words in a dictionary. For each word, write the guide words that appear on the page.

	Guide Words	
1. retreat	______	______
2. hawk	______	______
3. soldier	______	______
4. professor	______	______
5. business	______	______
6. dangerous	______	______
7. court	______	______
8. messenger	______	______
9. burst	______	______
10. quiver	______	______
11. winter	______	______
12. jungle	______	______

For each set of guide words, list three words that would appear on that page in a dictionary.

13. jacket–joy	**14. fat–feet**	**15. tail–toe**
______	______	______
______	______	______
______	______	______

DID YOU KNOW?

The earliest known dictionaries were written on clay tablets over 4,000 years ago. They were found in the ancient city of Elba.

Group Practice

Look up these words in a dictionary. For each word, write the guide words that appear on the page.

	Guide Words	
1. ordinary	______________	______________
2. skunk	______________	______________
3. knowledge	______________	______________
4. folk	______________	______________
5. ancient	______________	______________
6. waddle	______________	______________
7. information	______________	______________
8. terror	______________	______________
9. butter	______________	______________
10. gallop	______________	______________
11. thorn	______________	______________
12. dream	______________	______________
13. polish	______________	______________
14. racket	______________	______________
15. clover	______________	______________

For each set of guide words, list two words that would appear on that page in a dictionary.

16. dare–dinosaur ______________ ______________

17. sack–slam ______________ ______________

18. habit–heavy ______________ ______________

19. broom–butterfly ______________ ______________

20. pirate–plunge ______________ ______________

On Your Own

Look up these words in a dictionary. For each word, write the guide words that appear on the page.

Guide Words

1. funny ________________ ________________
2. laughter ________________ ________________
3. smile ________________ ________________
4. clown ________________ ________________
5. giggle ________________ ________________
6. happy ________________ ________________
7. cheerful ________________ ________________
8. playful ________________ ________________
9. wonderful ________________ ________________
10. delight ________________ ________________
11. grin ________________ ________________
12. chuckle ________________ ________________
13. riddle ________________ ________________
14. thrill ________________ ________________
15. outdoors ________________ ________________

For each set of guide words, list two words that would appear on that page in a dictionary.

16. battle–blizzard ________________ ________________
17. magazine–meal ________________ ________________
18. parachute–pen ________________ ________________
19. toad–tramp ________________ ________________
20. calm–celebrate ________________ ________________

LESSON 4 What Does It Mean?

WORDS TO KNOW

usage
the ways a word is used

slang
usage that is not widely accepted or known

standard
widely accepted usage

Class Practice

If you don't know what a word means, a dictionary can help. It gives the definitions of words. How a word is used is called **usage**. Sometimes word are used in ways that most people do not know or accept. That usage is called **slang**. Slang is not standard. **Standard** is the kind of writing used ir school work and books.

Look up the words printed in bold. For each word, circle the word t the right that matches its meaning best.

1. **orbit**	crazy	hole	path
2. **braid**	hair	weave	bandage
3. **design**	explanation	plan	hope
4. **shriek**	screech	jump	fear
5. **marsh**	flood	sheriff	swamp
6. **pair**	peel	two	equal
7. **fiery**	red	elf	burning

DID YOU KNOW?

Some words that were once slang are now standard: **bad-mouth, scram, hassle, nerd.** Be careful about using these words in your school work. Your teacher may still consider them slang!

Look up the words printed in bold. Find the word in the right column that matches its meaning best. Write that word in the blank

8. **entire**	____________	weak
9. **check**	____________	amount
10. **shallow**	____________	truthful
11. **measure**	____________	interest
12. **honest**	____________	perfect
13. **weep**	____________	arrest
14. **stake**	____________	bend

15. Look up the word **skinny**. Write its standard definition and its slang definition.

standard ____________

slang ____________

Group Practice

Look up the words printed in bold. For each word, circle the word to the right that matches its meaning best.

1. **hind**	front	rear	peel
2. **deed**	certain	agree	action
3. **skim**	remove	skate	steal
4. **mist**	cry	gone	spray
5. **rhythm**	move	beat	alike

Look up the words printed in bold. Find the word in the right column that matches its meaning best. Write that word in the blank.

6. **certain**	________________	upset
7. **fuss**	________________	habit
8. **knit**	________________	point
9. **practice**	________________	true
10. **spike**	________________	tie

Find the slang word in each sentence. Write that word in the first blank. In the second blank, write a standard word that has the same meaning.

11. The old actor was wearing a rug to look younger. ________________ ________________

12. Mia teased her brother about his new threads. ________________ ________________

13. Juan and Dave made plans to hang. ________________ ________________

14. Look up the word **cool**. Write its standard definition and its slang definition.

standard ________________________________

slang ________________________________

On Your Own

Look up the words printed in bold. For each word, circle the word to the right that matches its meaning best.

1. **reason**	right	idea	think
2. **pinch**	hit	squeeze	drink
3. **honor**	respect	badge	mean
4. **pit**	deep	toss	hole
5. **avoid**	escape	empty	direct

Look up the words printed in bold. Find the word in the right column that matches its meaning best. Write that word in the blank.

6. **list**	____________________	worn
7. **instrument**	____________________	tilt
8. **quarter**	____________________	pity
9. **drawn**	____________________	tool
10. **whittle**	____________________	destroy

Look up these words. For each word, write its standard definition and its slang definition.

11. **wheels**

standard____

slang ____

12. **dogs**

standard____

slang ____

13. **hip**

standard____

slang ____

LESSON 5 What Do You Mean, Exactly?

WORDS TO KNOW

context
the words surrounding a word in a sentence that can shed light on its meaning

Class Practice

The English language has thousands of words. Many words mean nearly the same thing, but not exactly. Think about the difference between the words **breathe** and **pant**. **Breathe** means to take air in and out of the lungs. **Pant** means to breathe quickly and hard. How do you know which word to use? A dictionary can help you find the words to say exactly what you mean. The **context** of the sentence can also help. Context means the other words around a word in a sentence.

Look up the words in each box. Then look at the context of each sentence. Decide which word fits better and write that word in the blank.

creep / crawl

1. The new parents were happy when their baby started to ____________.
2. The wolf crouched and began to ____________ toward the rabbit.

shrieked / shouted

3. The children ____________ when the thunder boomed.
4. The woman ____________ when the big dog ran through her flowers.

welcomed / saluted

5. The private stood up and ____________ the captain.
6. The mayor ____________ everyone who came to the meeting.

Look up the words in the box. Then look at the context of the sentence. Decide which word fits better and write that word in the blank.

called / cheered

7. When the last runner crossed the finish line, the crowd ____________.

looked / glanced

8. Tara carefully ____________ at all the used cars before buying one.

ate / gobbled

9. James ____________ his breakfast before racing out of the house to catch the bus.

squealed / creaked

10. The wheels of the rusty old wagon ____________.

Group Practice

Look up the words in each box. Then look at the context of each sentence. Decide which word fits better and write that word in the blank.

glared / stared

1. The cat ________________ at the hole in the log, patiently waiting for a mouse.
2. The little boy ________________ at the big boys who had taken his ball.

smiled / grinned

3. Everyone was happy when the sad little girl finally ________________.
4. The monkey ________________ and screeched when his keeper gave him a cookie.

pranced / paced

5. Waiting for his friend, Han ________________ around the room.
6. The famous white stallions ________________ across the field and bowed.

smell / stink

7. The ________________ from the rotten eggs filled the whole building.
8. The ________________ of fresh coffee drifted through the open window.

tapped / pounded

9. The woodpecker ________________ the dead tree to find insects.
10. The hard rain ________________ against the windows all night.

Look up the words in each box. Then look at the context of the sentence. Decide which word fits better and write that word in the blank.

breathe / pant

11. The couple paused to ________________ the fresh salty air from the ocean

bark / howl

12. The long ________________ in the middle of the night was frightening.

frightened / startled

13. The clatter of the falling books ________________ the sleeping student.

used / ancient

14. The scientists traveled to Egypt to study the ________________ ruins in the desert.

dipped / drooped

15. The colorful kite ________________ wildly in the wind.

DID YOU KNOW?

Ernest Hemingway rewrote the last page of his novel *A Farewell to Arms* thirty-nine times until he found the words to express exactly what he meant.

On Your Own

Rewrite the paragraph to make it more interesting. Use the words in the word list to take the place of the underlined words. Use your dictionary and the context to decide which words fit best.

WORD LIST				
knocked	bony	shouted	halted	peeked
humming	whipped	trudging	shining	worn
deserted	cast	colorless	crept	icy

The aged man walking up the empty street was tall and thin. The cold wind blew at the old man's long old coat. In the blowing snow, the street lights made a ghostly glow. The old man's pale lips seemed to curl into a smile. A soft, deep sound came from his throat. He stopped in front of the house. Light was coming through all of the windows. He looked through a window and spied the children inside. He slowly walked up the steps. He tapped loudly on the door with a thin hand. It opened slowly. Then the children called, "Happy birthday, Grandpa!"

LESSON 6 What's Another Word?

WORDS TO KNOW

synonym
a word that has the same or nearly the same meaning as another word

thesaurus
a book of synonyms

Class Practice

What's another word for happy? What's another word for sad? Words that mean nearly the same thing are called **synonyms**. A book that lists synonyms is called a **thesaurus**. A thesaurus can help you expand your vocabulary and make your writing more interesting.

Look up the words printed in bold in the thesaurus. Find a synonym for each word in the right column. Write that word in the blank.

1. faithful	________________	halt
2. strong	________________	loyal
3. nibble	________________	tough
4. bundle	________________	wrap
5. stop	________________	bite

Look up the underlined word in each sentence. Write a synonym over the underlined word. Use the words from the box.

strange
defend
voyage
gallop
blizzard

6. The soldiers prepared to <u>protect</u> the fort against the enemy.
7. The <u>journey</u> to the new land took three months.
8. The dark clouds and cold wind meant that a <u>storm</u> was coming.
9. The bear's loud growl made the horses break into a hard <u>run</u>.
10. The rock group was known for its <u>odd</u> costumes and wild behavior.

The word watched is used several times in this paragraph. Write a different synonym in each blank.

11. ________________ All morning, the farmer **watched** the sky with interest. Dark clouds rolled

12. ________________ in from the west. He **watched** one cloud that looked really threatening.

13. ________________ The cattle were restless, and the farmer **watched** the animals gather into a

14. ________________ tight bunch. He headed for cover. From the front porch, he **watched** the

15. ________________ rain cover the countryside. Then he went inside and **watched** television.

DID YOU KNOW?

The words *shirt* and *skirt* probably came from the same word, *skyrta*, in Old Norse. People living in different parts of Europe pronounced the word differently. The word became two different words with different meanings.

Group Practice

Look up the words printed in bold. Find a synonym for each word in the far right column. Write that word in the blank.

1. kayak	______________	mad
2. explore	______________	soft
3. salute	______________	canoe
4. protest	______________	blossom
5. crazy	______________	study
6. flower	______________	stout
7. stern	______________	foolish
8. tender	______________	polished
9. shiny	______________	object
10. silly	______________	greet

Look up the underlined word in each sentence. Write a synonym over the underlined word. Use the words from the box.

festival
tested
creepy
glad
slender

11. The children put on their costumes for the <u>carnival</u>.

12. The ballet dancer was <u>thin</u> and quick.

13. The travelers were <u>thankful</u> that the blizzard had ended.

14. The detective <u>examined</u> the steering wheel for fingerprints.

15. The space creatures in the movie were <u>dreadful</u>.

The word said is used several times in this paragraph. Write a different synonym in each blank.

16. ______________ At lunch, the friends were talking about the dance that night. Tina **said**

17. ______________ that she really liked the rock band. Peter **said** that he and Raul were going

18. ______________ early to help the band set up. Maria **said** that she would probably meet

19. ______________ them there a little late. Tina **said** that she would watch for Maria because a

20. ______________ huge crowd was expected. Raul **said** that he would take everyone home.

On Your Own

Look up these words. Write two synonyms for each.

1. bold ______________ ______________
2. express ______________ ______________
3. peaceful ______________ ______________
4. wonderful ______________ ______________
5. jumpy ______________ ______________
6. lonely ______________ ______________
7. run ______________ ______________
8. churn ______________ ______________
9. cord ______________ ______________
10. unite ______________ ______________

The word ran is used too many times in this paragraph. Write a different synonym in the blank each time.

Jose has a cat named Jingles. When Jose opened the front door, Jingles **ran 11.** ______________ outside. The cat **ran 12.** ______________ to the back of the house and then **ran 13.** ______________ under the porch. Jose **ran 14.** ______________ after his cat, calling its name. Just as Jose reached Jingles, the cat **ran 15.** ______________ up a tree. Jose started to climb the tree, but Jingles **ran 16.** ______________ back down. The cat **ran 17.** ______________ to the front of the house and through the open door. Jose **ran 18.** ______________ to close the door before Jingles could escape again. Jingles **ran 19.** ______________ up the stairs and **ran 20.** ______________ under the bed to hide.

LESSON 7 What's the Opposite?

WORDS TO KNOW

antonym
a word that means the opposite of another word

Class Practice

A thesaurus also lists antonyms. An **antonym** is a word that means the opposite of another word. Read these two sentences: **Those children are not polite** and **Those children are rude**. Which sentence is more forceful? Antonyms can make your writing stronger.

Use a thesaurus to find two antonyms for each word.

1. accept ____________ ____________
2. truth ____________ ____________
3. pity ____________ ____________
4. scold ____________ ____________
5. earnest ____________ ____________

These sentences do not make sense! Use a thesaurus to find an antonym for the bold word in each sentence. Then rewrite each sentence so that it makes sense.

6. The farmers in the area were hoping for a **skimpy** harvest this year.

   ____

7. The collector was excited to have found such a **common** coin!

   ____

8. The well-trained, gentle horse was a **pain** to ride.

   ____

9. After eating two **tiny** pizzas, Eric and Jake could hardly move.

   ____

10. Maria and Tina were **poor** students because they studied hard every night.

   ____

> **DID YOU KNOW?**
>
> The first edition of the *Thesaurus of English Words and Phrases* by Peter Mark Roget was published in 1852.

Group Practice

Look up the words in the first column. Then decide if the word in the second column is an antonym. If the words are antonyms, write yes**. If they are not antonyms, write** no**.**

1. start	introduce	______________
2. difficult	smooth	______________
3. support	protest	______________
4. grand	average	______________
5. distant	away	______________
6. enough	plenty	______________
7. plunge	dive	______________
8. custom	habit	______________
9. tough	tender	______________
10. faded	colorful	______________

Here are some more sentences that do not make sense! Use a thesaurus to find an antonym for the bold word in each sentence. Then rewrite each sentence so that it makes sense.

11. The class play was a sell-out every night and was a raging **failure**.

____

12. The good doctor was honored for her **selfish** work with children.

____

13. Julio received an award for playing the lead part in the play so **stiffly**.

____

14. The three **skinny** bakers obviously liked their own cooking.

____

15. When the team won the championship, all of the students felt very **ashamed**.

____

On Your Own

The same writer has been at it again! Use a thesaurus to find an antonym for the bold word in each sentence. Then rewrite each sentence so that it makes sense.

1. The **awkward** acrobat expertly tumbled and somersaulted across the floor.

   ____

2. The movie was so funny that everyone laughed **quietly**.

   ____

3. Marco was very **shy** and easily made friends with everyone.

   ____

4. The tired hikers sat around the **gloomy** fire and told ghost stories.

   ____

5. The **lazy** kitten played with the ball of yarn for hours every night.

   ____

The same writer wrote this paragraph, too. Cross out each of the bold words and write an antonym in the blank so that the paragraph makes sense.

That night, the **light** **6.** ______________ fog settled on the countryside like a blanket. In the dark and the fog, Cassie was driving **fast** **7.** ______________ along the narrow country road. Suddenly, a **scruffy** **8.** ______________ buck with **tiny** **9.** ______________ antlers appeared in the middle of the road. Cassie **tapped** **10.** ______________ on the brakes. The car slid to a stop. The deer bounded away. Clutching the steering wheel with **steady** **11.** ______________ hands, Cassie **calmly** **12.** ______________ pulled the car over to the side of the road. She breathed **shallowly** **13.** ______________ for a few minutes before she started on her way again.

LESSON 8 Just the Right Word

WORDS TO KNOW

phrase
a group of words

idiom
a phrase that does not mean what its individual words mean

Class Practice

The English language contains many phrases called idioms. A **phrase** is a group of words. An **idiom** is a phrase that does not mean exactly what the individual words mean. For example, to "hit the ceiling" means to become very angry. Someone who "hits the ceiling" does not really hit the ceiling with a fist! Idioms can be confusing if people do not know what they mean. Try to avoid using idioms in your writing.

Below is a list of several idioms and their meanings. A thesaurus gives you words or phrases to take the place of idioms in your writing. Using a thesaurus can make your meaning clearer.

A thesaurus also has lists of things that belong to a group. For example, it lists different types of sciences. Did you know that the study of bells is called **campanology**? A thesaurus also has the exact words for groups of animals. Did you know that a group of elk is called a **gang**? If your thesaurus does not have these lists, try the thesaurus in the library.

IDIOM	EXPLANATION
all eyes and ears	very interested
chew the fat	talk, discuss
blow one's top	become angry
in the doghouse	in trouble
call it a day	quit work
throw in the towel	give up
hit the sack	go to bed
jump the gun	be impatient
horse of a different color	something different
ball of fire	full of energy
break one's neck	try hard
cut the mustard	do a job
at the drop of a hat	immediately
down the drain	wasted
raise the roof	be noisy

The idioms in these sentences are underlined. Rewrite each sentence. Use the list to find a new word or phrase to take the place of the idiom.

1. When Kumiko told her story, we were all eyes and ears.

   ____

2. Every day, the old-timers met at the coffee shop to chew the fat.

   ____

3. Rufus was known for jumping the gun.

   ____

4. All the hours that the boys worked on the model were down the drain.

   ____

5. The girls were in the doghouse for eating all the cookies.

   ____

Group Practice

Rewrite the paragraph. Use a clearer word or phrase to take the place of each underlined idiom. Use the list on page 26 to help you.

> Shauna was trying to study for a test, but Lee and his friends were playing their music really loud and <u>raising the roof</u>. Shauna marched up to Lee's door. When he answered the door, Shauna said, "Stop playing your music so loud! If I don't make an A, I'll be <u>in the doghouse</u>!" Lee said, "Don't <u>blow your top</u>! I'll turn the music down right now. And I'm sorry." Shauna said, "I'm sorry, too." She went back to her apartment. After studying two more hours, she decided to <u>call it a day</u> and <u>hit the sack</u>.

____

____

____

____

____

____

____

____

____

____

Here are some kinds of sciences you should be able to find in a thesaurus. Write the exact name of each science in the blank. Use the list at the left to help you.

astronomy
zoology
ichthyology
speleology
meteorology
entomology

1. study of fish ______________________
2. study of weather ______________________
3. study of caves ______________________
4. study of animal life ______________________
5. study of stars and planets ______________________

On Your Own

Rewrite the letter. Use a new word or phrase to take the place of each underlined phrase.

> Dear Dr. Smith:
>
> I may be <u>jumping the gun</u>, but I am very interested in the <u>study of the stars and planets</u>. I would like to work for you because you are famous in this field. I am also very interested in the <u>study of animal life</u>, but that's <u>a horse of a different color</u>.
>
> My teachers say that I am a <u>ball of fire</u> when I decide to do something. I would <u>break my neck</u> to do a good job. I know that I can <u>cut the mustard</u>.
>
> Would you be willing to meet with me so that we can <u>chew the fat</u>? Just call me, and I will come <u>at the drop of a hat</u>.
>
> Sincerely,
>
> Jill Badwriter

____

____

____

____

____

____

____

____

Here are some groups of animals and birds. Write the exact name of each group in the blank. Use the list at the left to help you.

warren	**gang**
school	**litter**
bevy	**herd**
pride	**pod**
hive	**gaggle**

1. ______________ of fish

2. ______________ of quail

3. ______________ of elk

4. ______________ of geese

5. ______________ of lions

6. ______________ of whales

7. ______________ of puppies

8. ______________ of cattle

9. ______________ of rabbits

10. ______________ of bees

LESSON 9 Around the World—In Books

WORDS TO KNOW

research
the careful collection of information about a topic

reference book
a book of facts and information about one or more topics

topic
a subject; what a research paper is about

index
a list of topics and page numbers in a book

Class Practice

When you do **research**, you will need to use reference books. A **reference book** has facts and information about one or more **topics**. Information about almost any subject can be found in reference books. The **index** of a reference book can help you find the information you need. In most reference books, the index is at the back of the book. It lists topics and page numbers. The topics are listed in alphabetical order.

Here is part of an index from a reference book on trees. Use this example to answer Questions 1–3.

American elm **21–24**
bark 21
foliage 23
planting 24
pruning 24
Bald cypress **25–27**
bark 25
foliage 26
planting 27
Catalpa **28–30**
bark 28
foliage 29
planting 30

1. On what page could you learn about planting a catalpa tree? ______________
2. Which type of tree needs to be pruned? ______________
3. Which type of tree has the most information in this book? ______________

Encyclopedias have several volumes. Usually each volume is numbered and covers one or more letters of the alphabet. The index is usually in a whole volume by itself, and everything is listed in alphabetical order. Each entry is followed by the volume number and page number where the information can be found.

Here is an example from *Around the World Encyclopedia*. Use this example to answer Questions 4–6.

Carter, Jimmy (1924–), 39th president of the United States **4**:220
Begin **2**:125, *picture* **19**:66
Camp David Accords **5**:305, **9**:410
Carter Center, Emory University, *see in index* Carter Center

4. In which volume would you find information about Carter's presidency? ______________
5. In which volume and on which page would you find a picture of Carter and Begin? ______________
6. In which volumes would you find information about the Camp David Accords? ______________

DID YOU KNOW?

Encyclopedias date back to the time of Aristotle, an ancient Greek philosopher. In fact, he is sometimes called the "father of encyclopedias."

Group Practice

Here is another part of the index from the reference book on trees. Use the information from this index to answer these questions.

1. Which two major topics are discussed on the same pages?

____

2. Which major topic would give you information about topping a tree?

____

3. Which major topic takes up the most number of pages?

____

4. If you wanted to plant a fast-growing tree, on what pages should you look?

____

5. Which type of tree takes up the most number of pages?

____

6. On what pages would you find information on how often you should water a tree?

____

7. On what pages would you find information about pecan trees?

____

8. How many types of trees are listed?

____

9. On what pages would you find information about shade trees?

____

10. In this index, what are *Spraying*, *Watering*, and *Planting*?

____

On Your Own

Here is another part of the index from *Around the World Encyclopedia*. Use the information from this index to answer these questions.

Carter, Jimmy (1924–), 39th president of the United States **4:**220
- Begin **2:**125, *picture* **19:**66
- Camp David Accords **5:**305, **9:**410
- Carter Center, Emory University, *see in index* Carter Center
- Department of Education, **22:**435
- Department of Energy, **22:**437
- Ford **7:**330, **22:**411, *picture* **22:**412
- Georgia **8:**127
- Iran **9:**360
- Mondale **14:**315, *picture* **14:**317
- Nobel Peace Prize **15:**288
- Olympic Games of 1980 **15:**445
- Panama Canal Treaties **16:**75
- Reagan **18:**245
- Sadat 19:65, *picture* **19:**66
- Vietnam War **23:**280

1. In which volume and on what page would you find information about Carter's life in Georgia?

____

2. In which volume and on what page would you find information about Carter and Reagan?

____

3. Which two volumes have information on Carter and Ford?

____

4. Which four topics include pictures?

____

____

5. How many different volumes have information on Carter?

____

____

____

6. Which president was Jimmy Carter?

____

7. In what year was Carter born?

____

8. In which volume and on what page would you find information about the Nobel Peace Prize?

____

9. During which Olympics was Carter president?

____

10. Which two departments of government are listed in this index?

____

____

LESSON 10 Once More Around the World

WORDS TO KNOW

headline
the guide words in a reference book

photograph
a picture taken with a camera

illustration
an example of something in the form of a picture

caption
a title or explanation of a photograph, illustration, or map

subhead
a smaller heading used for a paragraph

Class Practice

Once you find a good article on your topic, you will want to make the most of the features in your reference book. Most reference books use **headlines, photographs, illustrations, captions, subheads,** and other features to get the information across. Here is a page from *Compton's Encyclopedia* that shows all of these features.

Use this example to answer the questions.

Headlines

Illustrations

Subheads

Captions

Photographs

110 ■ **EEL**

large mouths and teeth, and some are brightly colored or patterned. Morays grow to about 3.3 feet (1 meter) long, and some may even grow to about 10 feet (3 meters). Morays can become vicious when they are disturbed, and they may attack underwater divers.

Electric eels, members of the family Electrophoridae, belong to a group of fishes that is different from the other eels. They live in the fresh waters of South America. They are known for their capacity to generate an electric charge. The scientific name of the American freshwater eel is *Anguilla rostrata;* of the European species, *A. anguilla;* of the American conger, *Conger oceanicus;* of the European conger, *C. conger;* of electric eel, *Electrophorus electricus.* J. Whitfield Gibbons

EGG. All animals and plants, except for the most primitive types, begin their journey toward independent life when an egg is fertilized. An egg is a single female germ cell, or reproductive cell. It eventually develops into a new organism after it has been fertilized by a male germ cell (*see* Biology; Genetics). The egg cells of plants, when fertilized, develop into seeds (*see* Flower; Seed).

The development of a mammal begins when the female egg cell, or ovum, is fertilized by a male cell, or sperm. Very soon after fertilization the egg begins to divide. This process is called cleavage. The earliest stages of a mammal's development occur in its mother's body, from the time of fertilization until birth. In the early stages of development, a mammal is called an embryo. After specific external features are clearly formed, the unborn animal is referred to as a fetus. The developing human is called an embryo for the seven weeks following fertilization. Beginning in the eighth week it is called a fetus (*see* Embryology). The duckbill platypus and the spiny anteater are the only mammals that lay shelled eggs. All other mammals develop from shell-less eggs and remain inside their mothers' bodies until they are born.

A true egg, as distinguished from a shell-less egg cell, consists of the germ cell and materials that nourish the embryo, enclosed in a protective covering. These coverings may be a rigid shell made mostly of calcium carbonate, as in the eggs of birds, or they may be tough, elastic membranes, like those found on the eggs of most reptiles.

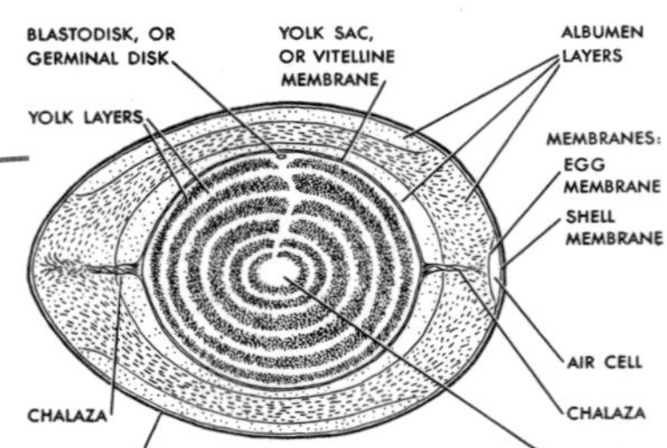

The yolk of a hen's egg cradles the germinal disk (blastodisk) from which the embryo chick develops, and it provides the embryo with food. Outside the yolk are the albumen, or egg white, and finally the shell. Each part is built in a series of concentric layers, and each is enclosed in protective sheaths. The chalazas are twisted strands of fiber that help to hold the yolk in the center of the egg. They are attached to the albumen at one end and to the yolk at the other.

All birds lay their eggs before the eggs are ready to hatch. Some snakes, lizards, fishes, and insects keep their eggs inside their bodies until the moment of hatching. The egg-laying habits of animals seem to be related to the dangers to which their eggs may be exposed. Hence, some birds that nest in remote places lay only one egg each season. But certain fishes, whose eggs become food for hundreds of enemies, lay millions of eggs at a time.

Many birds build elaborate nests in which they shelter their eggs (*see* Birds). The ways in which some insects protect their eggs are equally complicated. Bees and wasps lay eggs in specially constructed wax cells;

Hatching larvae (left) will become woolly bear caterpillars, then nocturnal moths. The king snake (center) coils around its eggs to keep them warm. Masses of frog eggs (right), laid in the water, may cling to plants or sink to the bottom.

(Left) E.S. Ross; (center) H.A. Thornhill—National Audubon Society Collection/Photo Researchers; (right) C.G. Maxwell—National Audubon Society Collection/Photo Researchers

1. What kind of snake does the middle photograph show?

____

2. What does the right photograph show?

____

3. What kind of egg is in the illustration?

____

4. What is the headline on this page?

____

5. What is the subhead on this page?

____

DID YOU KNOW?

The earliest photograph that is still in existence is called *View from the Window at Le Gras*. It was taken by Joseph Nicéphore Niépce in 1826.

Group Practice

Here is a page from the *Oxford American Children's Encyclopedia*. Use the information from this page to answer the questions.

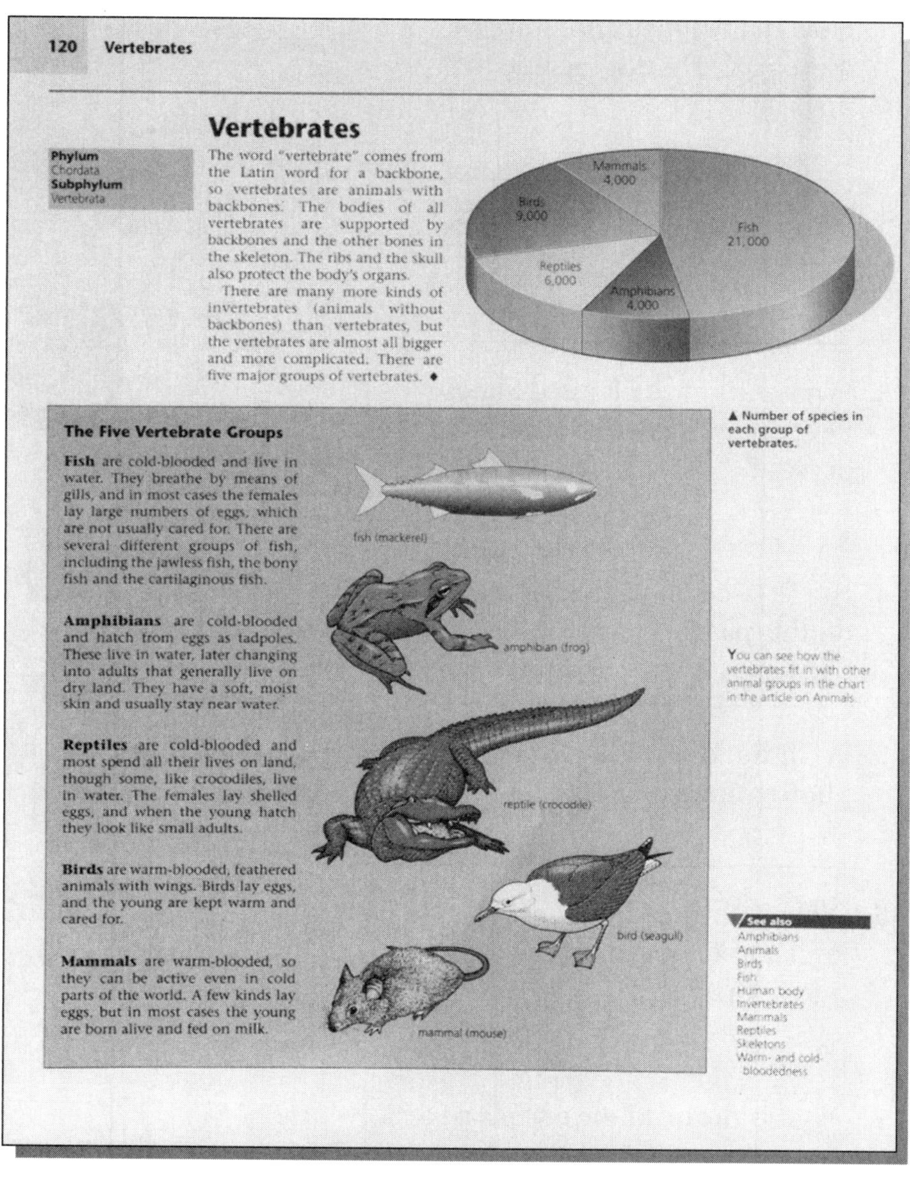

120 Vertebrates

Vertebrates

Phylum
Chordata
Subphylum
Vertebrata

The word "vertebrate" comes from the Latin word for a backbone, so vertebrates are animals with backbones. The bodies of all vertebrates are supported by backbones and the other bones in the skeleton. The ribs and the skull also protect the body's organs.

There are many more kinds of invertebrates (animals without backbones) than vertebrates, but the vertebrates are almost all bigger and more complicated. There are five major groups of vertebrates. ◆

▲ Number of species in each group of vertebrates.

The Five Vertebrate Groups

Fish are cold-blooded and live in water. They breathe by means of gills, and in most cases the females lay large numbers of eggs, which are not usually cared for. There are several different groups of fish, including the jawless fish, the bony fish and the cartilaginous fish.

Amphibians are cold-blooded and hatch from eggs as tadpoles. These live in water, later changing into adults that generally live on dry land. They have a soft, moist skin and usually stay near water.

Reptiles are cold-blooded and most spend all their lives on land, though some, like crocodiles, live in water. The females lay shelled eggs, and when the young hatch they look like small adults.

Birds are warm-blooded, feathered animals with wings. Birds lay eggs, and the young are kept warm and cared for.

Mammals are warm-blooded, so they can be active even in cold parts of the world. A few kinds lay eggs, but in most cases the young are born alive and fed on milk.

You can see how the vertebrates fit in with other animal groups in the chart in the article on Animals.

See also
Amphibians
Animals
Birds
Fish
Human body
Invertebrates
Mammals
Reptiles
Skeletons
Warm- and cold-bloodedness

1. What is the main topic on this page?

____

2. What is the headline on this page?

____

3. Write the subheads that appear on this page.

____

____

____

____

4. What is the caption of the illustration in the upper right corner?

____

____

____

5. According to the illustration in the upper right corner, how many species of reptiles are there?

____

On Your Own

Here is another page from *Compton's Encyclopedia*. Use the information on this page to answer the questions.

1. How many illustrations are on this page? (Do not include the map.)

   ____

2. What do all of the illustrations show?

   ____

3. What part of the United States is Oregon in —north, south, east, or west?

   ____

4. Name two subheads that appear on this page.

   ____

5. What building is shown in the photograph?

   ____

6. What is the heading for the information given on the right side of the page?

   ____

7. What is the headline on this page?

   ____

8. What is the caption for the illustration of the tree?

   ____

9. What is another name for Oregon?

   ____

582 ■ **OREGON**

State Symbols ***Facts About Oregon***

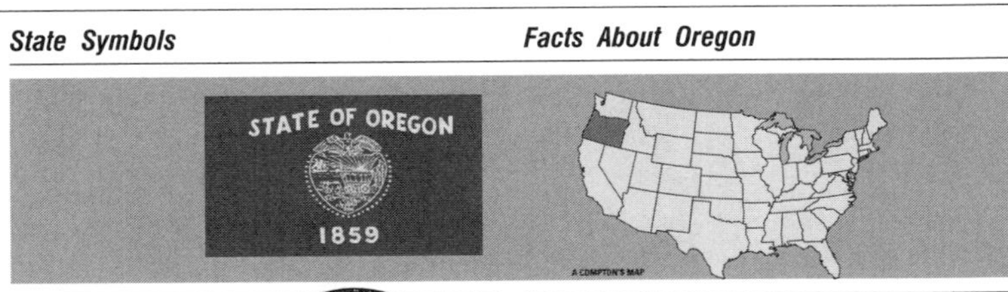

FLAG. Oregon's state flag, adopted in 1925, has the distinction of being the only state flag to be double-sided. On the front is the state escutcheon (shield) in gold on a blue field, surrounded by 33 stars. Above the escutcheon are the words "State of Oregon" and below it, the date 1859. On the back of the flag is a gold beaver, indicating the importance of that animal in the economy of the state.

SEAL. The seal of Oregon was designed by a legislative committee in 1857 and officially adopted in 1903. Oregon's pioneer heritage and rich natural resources are symbolized in various elements of the design: an elk, mountains, trees, a wagon, and the Pacific Ocean with a British man-of-war leaving as an American steamer arrives. A sheaf and a plow stand for agriculture and a pickax for mining. The shield is crested with an American eagle and bears the state motto, "The Union."

FISH. Chinook Salmon.

INSECT. Swallowtail Butterfly.

MAMMAL. Beaver.

ROCK. Thunderegg.

TREE: Douglas Fir

FLOWER: Oregon Grape

BIRD: Western Meadowlark

Nickname. Beaver State.

Motto. She Flies with Her Own Wings.

Song. 'Oregon, My Oregon', words by J.A. Buchanan and music by Henry B. Murtagh.

Entered the Union. Feb. 14, 1859, as the 33rd state.

Capital. Salem.

Population (2000 census). 3,421,399—rank, 28th state. Persons per square mile, 35.6 (persons per square kilometer, 13.8)—rank, 39th state.

Extent. Area, 97,132 square miles (251,571 square kilometers), including 1,050 square miles (2,720 square kilometers) of water surface (10th state in size).

Elevation. Highest, Mount Hood, 11,235 feet (3,424 meters), near Government Camp; lowest, sea level; average, 3,300 feet (1,006 meters).

Geographic Center. 25 miles (40 kilometers) southeast of Prineville.

Temperature. Extremes—lowest, –54° F (–48° C), Seneca, Feb. 10 1933, and on earlier dates at other locations; highest, 119° F (48° C), Pendleton, Aug. 10, 1898. Averages at Astoria—January, 40.4° F (4.7° C); July, 60.8° F (16.0° C); annual, 51.1° F (10.6° C). Averages at Medford—January, 37.4° F (3.0° C); July, 72.2° F (22.3° C); annual, 54.0° F (12.2° C). Averages at Pendleton—January, 30.8° F, (–0.7° C); July, 73.6° F (23.1° C); annual 52.2° F (11.2° C).

Precipitation. At Astoria—annual average, 77.43 inches (1,967 millimeters). At Medford—annual average, 19.55 inches (497 millimeters). At Pendleton—annual average, 12.60 inches (320 millimeters).

Land Use. Crops, 9.1%; pasture, 36.1%; forest, 43%; other, 11.1%.

(*See also* OREGON FACT SUMMARY.)

Oregon's marble and bronze State Capitol at Salem was completed in 1939. It is topped by a statue representing the hardy pioneers who settled the state in the mid-1800s.

Steve Terrill

LESSON 11 Read All About It!

WORDS TO KNOW

daily
every day

weekly
every week

section
a part, such as part of a newspaper

editorial
an article in a newspaper or magazine giving the writer's views

society
people in a community

classified advertisements
a section of a newspaper that lists jobs and things for sale

More Words to Know on page 36

Class Practice

Another good place to find information is a newspaper. Newspapers are printed **daily** or **weekly**.

Knowing the parts of a newspaper can help you find the information you need. A newspaper includes current news, advice, and articles about people and events. A large newspaper will also have several **sections**, or parts, such as world news, sports, **editorials**, **society**, and **classified advertisements**. In editorials, the newspaper writers express their views about things. The editorial section might also include letters to the editor. The society section of a newspaper gives local news about people and events in your city or town. Classified advertisements are also called **want ads**. This section lists jobs and things for sale.

Each section of a large newspaper is usually called by a letter, for example, section A. A large newspaper will also have a short index on the front or second page. The index lists the major sections of the paper and their page numbers. For example, the society section might start on page 1E.

The name of a newspaper is called the **banner**. For example, *The New York Times* is the name, or banner, of that paper. The banner appears on the front page in very large letters. At the very top of each page of a newspaper is a **running head**. The running head gives the name of the paper, the day of the week, the date, and the page number.

Thursday, November 17, 2005 Bigview Daily News, 2B

Bigview Mayor Fired!

AFTER several reports of illegal dealings, the mayor of Bigview, Janet Martin, was fired by the city council. Council members voted unanimously to fire the mayor after the city attorney, Jose Estevez, found evidence of crooked deals by Martin. The evidence includes tape recordings of Martin making deals with local businesses. Martin promised certain businesses that the city would buy their products or services at higher prices. Then Martin and the business owners could split the profit. Martin was not available for comment.

Several local businesses have been indicted. These include B & B Construction Company, All You Need Office Supplies, and Beautiful Lawns and Landscapes. The owners of all three businesses deny any wrongdoing. All of them claim to have been set up. The city attorney, however, has bank records showing checks made out by these business owners to the mayor.

The sums range from $5,000 to $20,000. The records also show that these deals had been going on for two years.

Use this example front page to answer these questions.

1. What is the banner of this newspaper?

   ____

2. What is the date of this newspaper?

   ____

3. How often does this newspaper come out?

   ____

WORDS TO KNOW

want ads
another name for classified advertisements

banner
the name of a newspaper

running head
name, day, date, and page number at the top of each page of a newspaper

Group Practice

Use this example to answer Questions 1–5.

Sunday, October 23, 2005 — Boomtown Bugler, **4D**

Boomtown Bobcats Go to State!

THE CROWD was in a frenzy last night when the Boomtown High School football team won the regional playoff game with a last-second field goal. Fans ran onto the field and carried all the players on their shoulders, cheering wildly. Later, many fans made up a parade, driving cars through the middle of town with horns blaring.

Coach Blair could not praise his players enough. He said that they had worked hard all season, putting in extra practices. He said they deserved to win and predicted that they would win the state playoff.

The team will face the Clearview Bears in the state championship game. The Bears played against the Junction Jaguars last night. The team's win was an upset because the Jaguars were favored to win the state championship.

The big game between the Bobcats and the Bears will be next Monday, October 31. It will take place at 2:00 P.M. at Midway City Stadium.

1. What is the banner of this newspaper?

____

2. What is the name of the section where this article probably appeared?

____

3. On what page does this article appear? _______________

4. What is the running head of this page?

____

5. What is the title of the article?

____

Use this example index to answer Questions 6–10.

INDEX

6. In what section would you look for a used car? _______________

7. What section would have news about a new state law?

____

8. On what page would you find what is showing at local theaters?

____

9. What page would have an article written by the editor of the paper? _______________

10. What section would have information about going to Mexico?

____

DID YOU KNOW?

The first daily newspaper in America was called the *Pennsylvania Packet and Daily Advertiser*. It started publication on September 21, 1784.

On Your Own

Use a copy of your local newspaper to answer these questions. Clip out the index to the paper and tape it to this page.

1. What is the banner of the newspaper?

   ___

2. What is the running head of the newspaper?

   ___

3. Find an article about your state's government. What is the title of the article?

   ___

4. What is the name of the section that has the article about state government?

   ___

5. Find an article that gives advice. What is the name of the article?

   ___

6. What is the name of the section that has the advice article?

   ___

7. On what page do editorials appear? ___

8. What is the name of the section that has the editorials?

   ___

9. What section has news about people who just got married?

   ___

10. What is the name of that section that has information about jobs?

    ___

Tape the index here.

LESSON 12 In the News

WORDS TO KNOW

opinion
someone's belief or view

fact
something that can be proved

factual
based on facts

Class Practice

An editorial is an article that expresses the writer's **opinion**. An opinion is a person's belief or view about something. Perhaps you do not like the color purple. That is your opinion. Purple is a mixture of blue and red. That is a **fact**. A fact is something that can be proved. A newspaper includes both **factual** information and opinions. If you use information from a newspaper in a research paper, you will want to make sure that the information is factual, not someone's opinion.

Here are two articles from the same newspaper about the same topic. Use these articles to answer the questions.

Lost Time

by J. J. Jackson

Every morning I drive to work along the same route, Highway 33. The total distance of my drive is ten miles. Of those ten miles, eight miles are under construction. The construction started three and one-half years ago, when the powers that be decided that the four-lane highway needed to be an eight-lane highway. In the meantime, what used to be four lanes is now two lanes. What used to take me 20 minutes of driving now takes me 35 minutes. Over the last three and one-half years, I have lost 420 hours to driving!

The powers that be say that the heavy traffic is something we have to put up with, just for a little longer. The construction should be completed, they say, in six months. That's another 60 hours of my time spent on the road.

Construction Nears Completion

by C. C. Calderas

People who regularly drive downtown know that eight miles of Highway 33 have been under construction since the fall of 2002. The city's Department of Public Services, the department in charge of streets, announced that the construction would be completed by October 2006. The announcement was made at the City Council meeting held last night.

This is good news for everyone who works downtown, including the people who work for the city. When the new part of the highway is completed, it will be a freeway. The 20 traffic lights that controlled traffic along those eight miles will be gone. The new part of the highway will be named Cochran Parkway, in honor of Dana Cochran, the mayor of Boomtown from 1990 through 1996.

1. What is the title of the editorial? ________________________

2. What opinion is the writer of the editorial trying to get across?

____

3. What opinion does the writer of the factual article have?

____

Group Practice

Use these two articles to answer the questions.

Local Horse Farm Raided

by Carl Early

The owners of Sunnyside Horse Farm, Ray and Betty Karnes, were arrested at their home on Friday, June 25. They were charged with 25 counts of animal abuse. The Kennedy County Sheriff, Ed Blackstone, received a tip from an unknown party about the conditions at the farm. Sheriff Blackstone and six of his deputies arrived at the farm, six miles out on Highway 45 East, at 6:00 in the morning. Sheriff Blackstone commented, "I just wanted to cry. I've never seen anything like it."

Local animal doctors and other good-hearted residents have come forward to help the horses. The doctors are providing free medicine and help to anyone who takes one of the horses to care for. Anyone interested in helping should call the sheriff's office at 210-555-1234.

It's a Shame!

by Paula Garcia

I don't believe we can punish the owners of Sunnyside Horse Farm too much. The images I saw on television last night made me sick. Following an anonymous telephone tip, the sheriff and his deputies raided the farm and found 25 horses dying from neglect and starvation.

Another really sad part of this story, besides the condition of the horses, is that the owners will only be fined $500 for each horse. That's not enough! I think the owners of that farm should be cooked "sunny side up"!

This incident is the third one this year. Perhaps the county leaders should pass a stronger law about animal abuse so that people who do such things are really punished.

1. Who is the writer of the news article?

____

2. List five facts in the news article.

____

____

____

____

____

3. What is the title of the editorial?

____

4. List three facts in the editorial.

____

____

____

DID YOU KNOW?

More than 1,500 daily newspapers are published in the United States.

On Your Own

Use these two articles from page 38 to answer the questions.

Lost Time

by J. J. Jackson

Every morning I drive to work along the same route, Highway 33. The total distance of my drive is ten miles. Of those ten miles, eight miles are under construction. The construction started three and one-half years ago, when the powers that be decided that the four-lane highway needed to be an eight-lane highway. In the meantime, what used to be four lanes is now two lanes. What used to take me 20 minutes of driving now takes me 35 minutes. Over the last three and one-half years, I have lost 420 hours to driving!

The powers that be say that the heavy traffic is something we have to put up with, just for a little longer. The construction should be completed, they say, in six months. That's another 60 hours of my time spent on the road.

Construction Nears Completion

by C. C. Calderas

People who regularly drive downtown know that eight miles of Highway 33 have been under construction since the fall of 2002. The city's Department of Public Services, the department in charge of streets, announced that the construction would be completed by October 2006. The announcement was made at the City Council meeting held last night.

This is good news for everyone who works downtown, including the people who work for the city. When the new part of the highway is completed, it will be a freeway. The 20 traffic lights that controlled traffic along those eight miles will be gone. The new part of the highway will be named Cochran Parkway, in honor of Dana Cochran, the mayor of Boomtown from 1990 through 1996.

1. List three facts in the editorial.

____

____

____

2. List five facts in the news article.

____

____

____

____

____

LESSON 13 The Magazine Rack

WORDS TO KNOW

periodical
something printed at regular times, such as newspapers and magazines

quarterly
printed four times a year

journal
a magazine

issue
a single printing of a magazine

More Words to Know on page 42

Class Practice

Magazines and newspapers are called **periodicals** because they come out at regular times. Some periodicals, such as newspapers, come out daily or weekly. Some magazines come out weekly or monthly. Other magazines come out only four times a year, or **quarterly**. A magazine is also called a **journal**. Magazines have short articles with up-to-date information about a wide range of topics. For this reason, magazines are a good place to find information for research.

Each printing of a magazine is called an **issue**. Some magazines have a **volume number** and an **issue number** to keep track of the issues. All magazines have a date. If a magazine comes out weekly, the date will include the month, day, and year. If a magazine comes out monthly, the date will have only the month and year. This information appears on the cover and sometimes on the page with the table of contents. When you do research, you will need to know this information so that you or someone else can find the information again.

Here is the table of contents page from an issue of *Crazy Sports.* Use it to answer Questions 1–5.

Crazy Sports

Volume 5, Number 3 **July 24, 2005**

From the Editor 8
From the Readers 9
Photos of the Week 11
Game of the Week 21
Will Will Go On? [Feature Article] 30
Too Much About Money!
[Feature Guest Article] 35
Will There Be Another Strike? 52
New Equipment for the Weekender 65
Sports Medicine: Doctors Needed! 72
Upcoming Events Around the World 82
A Rock-Climbing Horror Story 84
Designing Your Own Workout Room 95
Our Editor (the Duffer) Ranks the
Top Ten Courses 101

Crazy Sports July 24, 2005

1. How often does *Crazy Sports* come out?

   ____

2. What is the issue number? ____________

3. On what page does an article about new sports products start?

   ____

4. What is the title of the feature article?

   ____

5. Which article would tell you when the World Series starts?

   ____

WORDS TO KNOW

volume number
a number given to a set of magazines

issue number
a number given to a single printing of a magazine

Group Practice

Thousands of magazines are published in the United States and around the world. General interest magazines have information that nearly everyone is interested in. Other magazines are written for women, men, teenagers, or children. Some magazines are written for people interested in certain subjects, such as science, business, sports, music, or movies.

Here is a list of popular magazines. Use this list to answer the questions.

In Style	*National Geographic Magazine*	*People*
Reader's Digest	*Field & Stream*	*Time*
Discover	*Newsweek*	*Good Housekeeping*
Life	*Sports Illustrated*	*Popular Science*
Road and Track	*Fortune*	*TV Guide*
TV Guide		

1. List two magazines that are general interest magazines.

___

2. What magazine is probably about what people wear?

___

3. Which magazine will tell you what is showing on television?

___

4. Which magazine is probably about cars?

___

5. Which magazine is probably about money matters?

___

Use the magazine given to your group to answer these questions.

6. What is the title of the magazine?

___

7. How often is the magazine issued? ___

8. What is the date of the magazine? ___

9. What part of the public would read this magazine?

___

10. What is the general subject of this magazine, for example, general interest, science, sports?

___

On Your Own

Find two magazines from this list. Perhaps you have these magazines at home. If not, the school library or public library will have them. Use these magazines to answer the questions below.

National Geographic Magazine
Reader's Digest
Discover
Life
Road and Track
TV Guide
Field & Stream
Newsweek
Sports Illustrated
Fortune
People
Time
Good Housekeeping
Popular Science
In Style

Magazine 1

1. What is the title of the magazine?

____

2. How often is the magazine issued? _______________________

3. What is the date of the magazine? _______________________

4. What part of the public would read this magazine?

____

5. What is the general subject of this magazine, for example, general interest, science, sports?

____

Magazine 2

6. What is the title of the magazine?

____

7. How often is the magazine issued? _______________________

8. What is the date of the magazine? _______________________

9. What part of the public would read this magazine?

____

10. What is the general subject of this magazine, for example, general interest, science, sports?

____

LESSON 14 Don't Be a Word Thief

WORDS TO KNOW

plagiarism
copying or using another's work and passing it off as your own

cite
to name a source

source
the work where information was found

Class Practice

Plagiarism is copying or using another writer's work and passing it off as your own. Plagiarism is a form of stealing. When you use facts and ideas from someone else's work in your research, you must tell where you found the information. This is called **citing**, or naming, your **source**.

Here are two paragraphs. The first one is from a book written by Mark Searcher. It is the source. The second paragraph is from a student's paper.

> **Source**
>
> The journey has long been a basic form of storytelling. It was a way to give stories shape when humans first began to tell stories. The story of a journey appears in ancient writings, such as *The Odyssey* by Homer and *The Aeneid* by Virgil. The journey gave shape to the first novel ever written, *Don Quixote* by Cervantes. The journey itself can take many shapes. It can be the journey of a prince to save the fair princess. It can be the journey of a knight to kill a dragon. It can be the story of a hero who is trying to save his friends. In all these types of journeys, the hero must face many dangers.

> **Student Paper**
>
> Writers shape their stories in many different ways. One way is the journey. Humans have long used the journey to give their stories shape. Some famous novels are about journeys. One is *Huckleberry Finn* by Mark Twain. Huck tries to help his friend Jim. Huck and Jim face many dangers. Some of their experiences are funny, but most are truly dangerous.

Write the sentences and ideas in the student's paper that are taken from the source.

____

____

____

____

____

Group Practice

For each set of sentences, decide if the idea in the paper is the same as the idea in the source and the student would need to credit the source. Write yes if the ideas are the same. Write no if they are not.

Source	Student Paper	Yes or No
1. Part of the movie *Titanic* is based on fact, and part of it is fiction.	My favorite movie of all time is *Titanic* because of its special effects.	
2. Cats were first made into household pets by the ancient Egyptians more than 4,000 years ago.	The cat has very good vision and hearing and the ability to learn. My cat is a good example.	
3. Amelia Earhart was the first American woman to fly across the Atlantic Ocean alone.	Amelia Earhart was a famous American woman pilot.	
4. Larry McMurtry's two best novels are *Horseman, Pass By* and *Lonesome Dove*.	*Lonesome Dove* is about a cattle drive from Texas to Montana and is one of Larry McMurtry's best novels.	
5. Hemingway based the main character, Santiago, in *The Old Man and the Sea* on an old man he knew in Cuba.	The main character in *The Old Man and the Sea* is based on an old man Hemingway actually knew.	
6. The president of the United States is elected every four years.	The U.S. president is the head of one of the most powerful nations in the world.	
7. John Glenn was the first American astronaut to orbit the earth.	The first American astronaut to orbit the earth was John Glenn.	
8. Most movies today are made for young people, from ages 15 through 30.	There are five movie ratings: G, PG, PG-13, R, and NC-17.	
9. The play and movie *West Side Story* are based on Shakespeare's play, *Romeo and Juliet*.	*Romeo and Juliet* by Shakespeare is a very sad love story.	

On Your Own

For each set of sentences, decide if the idea in the paper is the same as the idea in the source and the student would need to credit the source. Write yes if the ideas are the same. Write no if they are not.

	Source	Student Paper	Yes or No
1.	Ernest Hemingway based many of his novels on his own life experiences.	In his novels, Hemingway wrote about many of his own experiences.	
2.	In 1927, Charles Lindbergh made the first solo flight across the Atlantic Ocean.	The plane that Lindbergh flew across the Atlantic in 1927 was called "The Spirit of St. Louis."	
3.	The Mississippi River starts in Minnesota and flows for 2,340 miles and then empties into the Gulf of Mexico.	The Mississippi River runs from Minnesota to the Gulf of Mexico. It is 2,340 miles long and is the longest river in the United States.	
4.	Country-western music has its roots in the folk songs of the people who live in the Appalachian Mountains.	American country-western music is popular around the world, from the United States to China.	
5.	In 1947, Chuck Yeager was the first pilot to break the sound barrier.	At sea level, sound travels about 760 miles per hour.	
6.	One of the most famous paintings in the world is the *Mona Lisa* by Leonardo da Vinci.	Leonardo da Vinci painted one of the most famous paintings in the world.	

DID YOU KNOW?

George Harrison of the Beatles was guilty of plagiarism. He used the music from the song "He's So Fine" by the Chiffons for his song "My Sweet Lord."

Here are two paragraphs. The first one is from a book written by Stephen Hawking in 1980. The second paragraph is from a student's paper. Underline the sentences in the student's paper that are the same ideas as in the source.

Source

I was seventeen, and most of the other students in my year had done military service and were a lot older. I felt rather lonely during my first year and part of the second. It was only in my third year that I really felt happy there.

Student Paper

When people are in a new place, they can feel very lonely, even when they are surrounded by other people. One of my heroes, Stephen Hawking, had that feeling when he went away to college. He said that he had been lonely during his first year and part of the second. I was having that feeling during my first year at college. I knew things would get better, just like they did for Stephen. He had been happy in his third year. Remembering that made me feel better. If he could do it, so could I.

LESSON 15 Cite Your Sources

WORDS TO KNOW

quotation marks
marks that surround words taken directly from a source

bibliography
a list of sources used in a research paper

entry
a single source listed in a bibliography

Class Practice

You must cite your sources in two places in your paper. First, cite a source inside your paper, where you use the words or ideas. Put the writer's last name and the copyright year of the source in parentheses. Here is an example.

> For example, *The Odyssey* by Homer is about a journey (Searcher, 1993).

If you use the **exact** words of another writer, put **quotation marks** around those words. Also include the page number of the source where you found the words. Here is an example. The writer's last name, the year, and the page number of the source are all in the parentheses.

> The journey "was a way to give stories shape when humans first began to tell stories" (Searcher, 1993, p. 15).

The second place you must cite your sources is the **bibliography** at the end of your paper. A bibliography is an alphabetical list of the sources that you used. Each source listed in your bibliography is called an **entry**. Each kind of source follows a certain form. Here are the forms for a book, a magazine article, a newspaper article, and an encyclopedia article.

Type of Source	Example
Book Writer's Last Name, Writer's First Name. *Title of Book*. City of Publication: Publisher. Copyright Date.	Hemingway, Ernest. *The Old Man and the Sea*. New York: Charles Scribner's Sons. 1952.
Magazine Article Writer's Last Name, Writer's First Name. "Title of Article." *Title of Magazine*. Date or Volume Number, Issue Number: Page Numbers.	Crooks, Alan F. "Larry McMurtry: A Writer in Transition." *Western American Literature*. Volume 7: 151–155.
Encyclopedia Article Writer's Last Name, Writer's First Name. "Title of Article." *Title of Encyclopedia.* Copyright Date. Volume Number: Page Numbers.	Aschmann, Homer. "Paraguay". *Compton's Encyclopedia*. 2000. Volume 18: 547–553.
Newspaper Article Writer's Last Name, Writer's First Name. "Title of Article." *Title of Newspaper*. Date: Page Numbers.	Revkin, Andrew. "Scientists Chart Twisters." *San Antonio Express-News*. November 18, 2002: 6F.

HELPFUL HINT

Instead of using italics for the title of a book or magazine, underline the title: The Old Man and the Sea. This can be very useful when you are writing notes by hand.

Group Practice

Here are three quotations and their sources. Rewrite each quotation and cite the source the way they should appear inside a paper.

1. Then he began to pity the great fish that he had hooked. From the book *The Old Man and the Sea*, page 48, by Ernest Hemingway, 1952.

2. Maycomb was an old town, but it was a tired old town when I first knew it. From the book *To Kill a Mockingbird*, page 11, by Harper Lee, 1960.

3. I was getting on in years, well into my thirties and I couldn't stand these shocks like I used to. From the book *Every Living Thing*, page 3, by James Herriot, 1992.

HELPFUL HINT

For a book or article with a writer's name, alphabetize by the writer's last name.

If a writer's name is not given for an article, alphabetize by the first word in the title of the article.

When you use the title of an article to alphabetize, pretend that the words *a*, *an*, and *the* are not there.

Here is the information for these three sources. Rewrite them in correct form and in alphabetical order for a bibliography. Use the examples on page 47 to help you.

The Old Man and the Sea by Ernest Hemingway. Published in 1952 by Charles Scribner's Sons in New York, New York.

To Kill a Mockingbird by Harper Lee. Published in 1960 by J.B. Lippincott Company in Philadelphia, Pennsylvania.

Every Living Thing by James Herriot. Published in 1992 by St. Martin's Press in New York, New York.

On Your Own

Here are five sources for another paper. Rewrite them in correct form for a bibliography. Be sure to put them in alphabetical order. Use the examples on the page 47 to help you.

Mark Twain's book *Roughing It* published in New York, New York, by Penguin Books in 1985

A book called *The Trail-Driving Rooster* published in 1955 by Harper & Brothers, of New York, New York, and written by Fred Gipson

The First Salute, a book by Barbara W. Tuchman, published in 1988 by Alfred A. Knopf of New York, New York

An article called "At the High End of the River" by Diane Young on pages 126–131 of the June 2000 issue of the magazine *Southern Living*

A newspaper article called "Holidays of Yore," on page 1B in the *San Antonio Express-News*, dated December 28, 2002, by Scott Huddleston

DID YOU KNOW?

Harry S. Truman was the 33rd president of the United States. After he graduated from high school and before he became president, he read history books and encyclopedias in his spare time.

LESSON 16 Get to the Point

WORDS TO KNOW

skim
to look quickly for a particular piece of information

scan
to read quickly to find out what something is generally about

main idea
a statement of what an article is about

summary
the point about the main idea that the writer is trying to make

Class Practice

When you **skim** an article, you quickly look for a particular item, such as a name or date. When you **scan** an article, you quickly read it to discover what it is generally about. For example, you skim and scan when you look up a number in a telephone book. First, you skim the columns to find the first letter of a friend's last name. Then, when you get close to the information you are looking for, you read more carefully to find your friend's name and number.

Decide whether you should skim and scan or read carefully to do each exercise. Write skim & scan or read carefully in the blank.

1. Know how to do a science experiment ____________________
2. Find a page number in a table of contents ____________________
3. Understand a story for English class ____________________
4. Find the name of a particular character in a story ____________________
5. Find out what a bald eagle looks like____________________

Skim a page to find subheads, key words at the start of paragraphs, and captions under illustrations. These will give you a good idea of what the article is about. If the article has information you can use, then read it carefully. Write down the bibliography information. Also write down the **main idea** and a **summary** of the information. A summary is written in your own words and is as short as possible. Here is an example article, the main idea, and a summary.

> The horse first began in North America around 50 million years ago and spread to other parts of the world. Then, about 10,000 years ago, the horse died out in North America. In the 1500s, Spanish explorers brought horses with them to Mexico. The mustangs that roam the western United States came from those horses.

Main Idea: Mustang horses in the western United States live where horses first began.

Summary: Millions of years ago, the horse began in North America but died out. Spanish explorers brought horses back to North America. The mustangs of the western U.S. come from those horses.

Group Practice

Here are two short articles. Write the main idea and a summary for each one.

Tunnels are underground passages that are used for many different purposes. For example, the subway trains in New York City travel through a large network of tunnels. Some tunnels are used by cars and trucks to travel through mountains. The longest mountain tunnel in the world is in Norway. It is 15.2 miles long. Other tunnels are used by trains. Perhaps the most famous train tunnel is the Channel Tunnel. The Channel Tunnel is 31 miles long. It lies beneath the English Channel and connects England and France. Other tunnels are used to carry water from one place to another. The Delaware Aqueduct in the United States is used for this purpose. In fact, the Delaware Aqueduct is 85 miles long, the longest tunnel in the world!

Main Idea: ______________________________

____

Summary: ______________________________

____

____

____

____

____

Chocolate is a favorite flavor around the world. It is used for candy, ice cream, cakes, cookies, and chocolate milk. The Aztecs were the first people to use cocoa beans to make a chocolate drink, called *chocolatl.* Only the members of the Aztec royal family were allowed to drink it. But they did not use sugar. Spanish explorers took cocoa beans back to Europe. Europeans added sugar to make a sweet drink. People started experimenting with cocoa to make the sweet chocolate treats we like to eat today. Scientists have studied chocolate to find out why people love it. They still do not know chocolate's mystery.

Main Idea: ______________________________

____

Summary: ______________________________

____

____

____

____

____

DID YOU KNOW?

Before radio, telephones, and computers were invented, ships used flags to communicate with each other. Each position of a flag meant a different letter. Today, ground crews in airports and on aircraft carriers still use flags to communicate with pilots.

On Your Own

Here are two short articles. Write the main idea and a summary for each one.

The Amazon River in South America is the second longest river in the world and is a place of wonder and mystery. It starts in the Andes Mountains of Peru and flows for 4,007 miles to the coast of Brazil. It is so large and deep that ocean ships can travel up the river nearly 1,000 miles. It is the home of many different and strange animals and plants, such as the piranha fish. The largest water lily in the world, which can grow to six feet wide, grows in the Amazon. Much of the land around the Amazon River has never been explored. Native peoples who live in the forests still live the way they did hundreds of years ago.

Main Idea: ____________________

____

Summary: ____________________

____

____

____

____

____

Mark Twain is sometimes called the greatest American writer. Most of us are familiar with his stories, such as *Huckleberry Finn*, *The Adventures of Tom Sawyer*, and "The Jumping Frog of Calaveras County." On the surface, the stories are funny. We laugh when Huck Finn dresses up as a girl to disguise himself, and we chuckle when Tom Sawyer persuades his friends that painting a fence is great fun. But on a deeper level, Mark Twain's stories are also very serious. Twain thought that some things in American society were wrong and used his stories to say so. For example, *Huckleberry Finn* is set in the United States before the Civil War. The story shows how wrong slavery was. Huck helps Jim, a slave, escape his owners so that he will not be sold and taken away from his family.

Main Idea: ____________________

____

Summary: ____________________

____

____

____

____

____

LESSON 17 Make a Note of It

Class Practice

After you have found several articles on your research topic, the next step is to reread the articles and take careful notes. Your notes should include the bibliographic information, the main idea, a summary, and details that support the main idea. You should also include quotations that you might want to use in your paper. Write down words that you do not know so that you can write their definitions in your notes. Here is an example.

> Humans can turn simple things into works of art. A certain type of sand, called silica, is melted at high heat and turned into glass objects. Clay is a type of soil that is formed into beautiful pottery. Thin strips of bamboo, a type of jungle plant, are woven into intricate baskets. Even wool from sheep is dyed beautiful colors and woven into rugs.

Main Idea: Humans make art from plain materials.

Summary: Humans turn melted sand, clay, bamboo, and wool into works of art.

Details: melted sand, or silica, made into glass objects
clay made into pottery
bamboo made into baskets
wool woven into rugs

Here is an article about football. Write the main idea, a summary, and supporting details.

> Football has a very long history. A type of football was played in ancient Greece thousands of years ago! There are also many types of modern football. Besides American football, there is Canadian football, Australian football, and Gaelic football. Even soccer and rugby are forms of football. Each type has different rules, and the rules have changed many times over the years. Even so, all of the different types of football have the same basic idea: to get the ball across the other team's goal line.

Main Idea: ____________________

Summary: ____________________

____

Details: ____________________

____

____

Group Practice

Here are two articles. Write the main idea, a summary, and supporting details for each. Be sure to look up words you do not know and write their definitions.

> Hot air balloons were first invented as a way to travel. However, sport ballooning grew in popularity, especially in the United States, in the 1980s and 1990s. One of the greatest hot air balloon shows is the yearly International Balloon Fiesta in Albuquerque, New Mexico. The first nonstop trip around the world in a hot air balloon was made in 1999. It took the balloonists a little over nineteen days. This idea is not new. In 1873, Jules Verne wrote a book about it called *Around the World in Eighty Days*.

Main Idea: ______________________________

Summary: ______________________________

____

____

Details: ______________________________

____

____

____

____

> Many things that people needed for everyday life used to be made by hand. This included candles for light, quilts to keep warm, saddles for riding horses, shoes, clothes, soap for bathing, and furniture. Today, these things can be made quickly and cheaply by machines. But hand-made things are highly valued, and they can be very expensive. People pay hundreds of dollars for handmade saddles, boots, hats, and belts. Towns everywhere have yearly shows of handmade quilts. Many shops that carry fancy candles charge more for candles carved by hand.

Main Idea: ______________________________

Summary: ______________________________

____

____

Details: ______________________________

____

____

____

____

DID YOU KNOW?

Movable type was probably invented by Johannes Gutenberg in 1450. Before that, books and anything else that was written had to be copied by hand.

On Your Own

Here are two articles. Write the main idea, a summary, and supporting details for each. Be sure to look up words you do not know and write their definitions.

Our ideas of the cowboy's life come mostly from movies. The cowboy is usually seen as an American hero. But the life of the cowboy was not very wonderful. He worked hard for someone else and had little to show for it. He usually owned only a few clothes, his horse, and his saddle. His main job was rounding up and driving cattle to market. Cattle drives took from days to months. The cowboy lived a lonely life. Other cowboys were his only family. He could not afford to marry and have children. His only home was a bunkhouse or the open range.

Main Idea: ______________________________

Summary: ______________________________

____

____

Details: ______________________________

____

____

____

____

Perfume-making is a world-wide, multi-million dollar business. Perfume is popular with girls and women of all ages. In the last twenty-five years, perfume for men has also become extremely popular. The latest trend is perfume to be used by both men and women. It is called "unisex" perfume. Perfume is usually liquid, but it can also be in the form of oil, lotion, or cream. Perfumes range from musky and spicy scents to light floral scents.

Main Idea: ______________________________

Summary: ______________________________

____

____

Details: ______________________________

____

____

____

____

LESSON 18 Meet Me at the Library

Class Practice

Now, where can you find the information that you need? The library is a good place to start. There are many types of libraries. Your school has its own library. Most towns and cities have a public library. Public libraries serve many different people, from children to senior citizens. They offer programs and services for every age group. Many public libraries also have free Internet access.

When you walk into a library for the first time, you might feel a little lost. Where do you start? Most libraries have sections. Each section has a different type of material. Here are the sections that most school libraries have and the kinds of materials you can find in each one.

Fiction Books	Books that tell stories drawn from the writer's imagination
Nonfiction Books	Books about things that actually happened
Biographies	Books written about actual people's lives A book written by a person about his or her own life is called an **autobiography**. Diaries are a type of autobiography.
Reference Books	Books that provide particular information, such as dictionaries, encyclopedias, and thesauruses
Periodicals	Magazines and newspapers
Multimedia	Audiocassettes, videocassettes, CD-ROMs, and Internet access

Fill in the blank with the name of the library section where you could find these materials.

1. *The Hobbit* by J.R.R. Tolkien ____________________

2. *The New York Times* newspaper ____________________

3. *Dictionary of Slang and Unconventional English* ____________________

4. a film about the great white shark ____________________

5. *The Autobiography of Malcolm X* ____________________

6. *Mexico: A History in Art* ____________________

DID YOU KNOW?

In 1731, Benjamin Franklin founded the first public library in America. It was called the Philadelphia Library.

Group Practice

Here is a library cart full of books and other materials. They are a mess and need to be put back where they belong. List all the materials that belong under each library section.

an issue of *People Magazine*

Crazy Horse by Larry McMurtry

an audiocassette of *Little Women*

Roget's International Thesaurus

an issue of *Rolling Stone Magazine*

Anne Frank: Diary of a Young Girl

Dictionary of American Regional English

Forrest Gump by Winston Groom

a book on the War of 1812

a film on clipper ships

Yeager by Chuck Yeager

a copy of the *Wall Street Journal*

a videocassette of *Moby Dick*

A History of the Western World

Catch-22 by Joseph Heller

Periodicals

____

____

____

____

Reference

____

____

____

____

Multimedia Center

____

____

____

____

Fiction Books

____

____

____

____

Nonfiction Books

____

____

____

____

Biography

____

____

____

____

DID YOU KNOW?

When the Library of Congress was burned by British troops during the War of 1812, Thomas Jefferson replaced the library with his own personal library.

On Your Own

Find each of these materials in the library. List each one in bibliographic form under the library section where you found it. One has been done for you.

an article about sports from a local newspaper

an article from a popular magazine

an article from an encyclopedia

a dictionary

an autobiography

a biography of a person from American history

a nonfiction book

another nonfiction book

a fiction book

another fiction book

Periodicals

____

____

____

____

____

Reference

____

____

____

____

____

Multimedia Center

____

____

____

____

____

Fiction Books

____

____

____

____

____

Nonfiction Books

Boorstin, Daniel. The Discoverers.

New York: Vintage Books. 1985.

____

____

____

Biography

____

____

____

____

____

LESSON 19 Find Your Way: Periodical Indexes

WORDS TO KNOW

periodical index
a publication that lists magazine articles by subject and author

abbreviation
a short form of a word

Class Practice

When you do research, you can find basic information on your topic in encyclopedias and other reference books. What if you want the latest information on your topic? Magazines provide up-to-date information on a wide range of subjects. Magazines have information on subjects from popular music to new discoveries in medicine. How can you find articles on your topic without reading all the magazines ever printed? A **periodical index** lists articles by subject and author. For example, the article "A Balanced Diet" would not be listed under the title. It would be listed under subjects such as "health," "diet," and "nutrition." Here is part of a page from a periodical index.

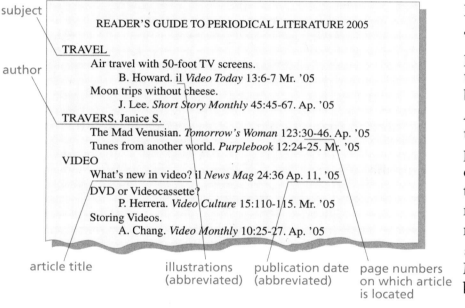

READER'S GUIDE TO PERIODICAL LITERATURE 2005

TRAVEL
Air travel with 50-foot TV screens.
B. Howard. il *Video Today* 13:6-7 Mr. '05
Moon trips without cheese.
J. Lee. *Short Story Monthly* 45:45-67. Ap. '05
TRAVERS, Janice S.
The Mad Venusian. *Tomorrow's Woman* 123:30-46. Ap. '05
Tunes from another world. *Purplebook* 12:24-25. Mr. '05
VIDEO
What's new in video? il *News Mag* 24:36 Ap. 11, '05
DVD or Videocassette?
P. Herrera. *Video Culture* 15:110-115. Mr. '05
Storing Videos.
A. Chang. *Video Monthly* 10:25-27. Ap. '05

subject
author
article title
illustrations (abbreviated)
publication date (abbreviated)
page numbers on which article is located

The subject or author's name is printed in capital letters. Articles about that subject or by the author are listed below it in alphabetical order by title. All of the bibliographic information that you need to find the article is provided. The entry includes the title of the article, the author, the name of the magazine, the volume and page numbers, and date. But what does *Mr.* mean? That is a shortened name, or an **abbreviation,** for the month of March. A periodical index saves space by using abbreviations.

Here are some questions. List the subjects you might look under in a periodical index to find articles to answer each question.

1. What equipment does a person need for rock climbing? ____________

____

2. What is life like for the average Russian today? ____________

____

3. What are the latest discoveries from space exploration? ____________

____

DID YOU KNOW?

One of the first American periodicals was *General Magazine and Historical Chronicle*. It started in 1741. It was published by Benjamin Franklin.

Group Practice

Use the periodical index given to your group to do this exercise. Be sure to use complete bibliographic form to list the articles. Here is a guide to help you.

> Writer's Last Name, Writer's First Name. "Title of Article." *Title of Magazine*. Date or Volume and Issue Numbers: Page Numbers.

For each question, list three articles that might answer the question. To the right of each article, write the subject it was listed under.

1. What are the effects of loud music on hearing?

______________________________ ____________

____

______________________________ ____________

____

______________________________ ____________

____

2. What are American farmers doing to grow better vegetables?

______________________________ ____________

____

______________________________ ____________

____

______________________________ ____________

____

3. Besides gas, what else can cars run on?

______________________________ ____________

____

______________________________ ____________

____

______________________________ ____________

____

On Your Own

Choose a topic in science that interests you. Find five articles in a periodical index about your topic. To the right of each article, write the subject it was listed under.

____ ________________

____

____ ________________

____

____ ________________

____

____ ________________

____

____ ________________

____

Find one of the articles that you listed. Read the first paragraph of the article. Write the main idea, a summary, and details for that paragraph.

Main Idea: ____

____

Summary: ____

____

____

____

Details: ____

____

____

____

____

LESSON 20 Find Your Way: Fiction

WORDS TO KNOW

fiction
a story drawn from the writer's imagination

novel
a fiction book

genre
kind of book or short story

Class Practice

Fiction is a story drawn from the writer's imagination. Fiction can take many forms. It can be in the form of a short story, such as "The Stolen White Elephant" by Mark Twain. It can be in the form of a book, called a **novel**, such as *Forrest Gump* by Winston Groom. There are many different kinds, or **genres**, of novels and short stories. Here are descriptions of some of the genres of fiction you will find in the library.

- **Historical** or **Realistic Fiction:** Historical or realistic novels are set in an actual time and place with make-believe characters.
- **Science Fiction:** This kind of novel is often set in the future, on another planet, or in an imaginary time or place. It often answers the question "What if . . . ?" For example, "What if we could travel in time?" has been the basis for many science fiction novels.
- **Mystery:** A mystery sets up a problem that must be solved. The problem might be a crime or a strange happening. There are many kinds of mysteries. A detective story is one kind and is sometimes called a *whodunit*. Other kinds of mysteries are spy novels and scary stories.
- **Fantasy:** A fantasy is a story that takes place in a world that is not real. The characters are also unreal. Fairy tales are one kind of fantasy story. Fantasies often have dragons, castles, wizards, magic forces, and knights who fight against forces of evil.

Here is a list of novels and a short description of each. Write the genre of each in the blank.

1.	*A Wrinkle in Time*	Meg travels to a distant planet to set her father free.	________
2.	*The Westing Game*	In this whodunit, the character who identifies the guilty person first receives a fortune.	________
3.	*The Hobbit*	Bilbo Baggins sets out to find a treasure that a dragon stole long ago.	________
4.	*Gone With the Wind*	Set during the American Civil War, a young woman, Scarlett O'Hara, must deal with the effects of war.	________

Group Practice

Here is a list of titles of novels, the writers' names, and short descriptions. Write the genre of each novel in the blank.

	Title	Writer	Description	Genre
1.	*The Once and Future King*	T. H. White	Story of King Arthur and the knights of the Round Table	____________
2.	*Red Badge of Courage*	Stephen Crane	Story of a young man's reactions during the American Civil War	____________
3.	*Little Women*	Louisa May Alcott	The four March sisters grow into young women during the 1800s.	____________
4.	*And Then There Were None*	Agatha Christie	Ten people on an island are killed one by one. Who is the killer?	____________
5.	*The Time Machine*	H. G. Wells	George invents a time machine that allows him to travel into the future.	____________
6.	*Bolt*	Dick Francis	Who is killing the prize racehorses?	____________

Novels are placed on the library shelves in alphabetical order by the writer's last name. Place these novels in order. Write the writer's last name and first name and the title of each novel. The first one has been done for you.

7. Alcott, Louisa May. Little Women

8. ____

9. ____

10. ____

11. ____

12. ____

DID YOU KNOW?

The novel *Tom Jones* was written in 1749 by Henry Fielding. Part of it is a mystery. Tom must discover his real parents.

On Your Own

Sometimes you can learn what kind of novel a book is by reading the inside of the book jacket. Sometimes the books are grouped by genre in the library.

You must go to the library to complete this scavenger hunt! Find each of these books on the library shelves. Be sure to write your answers in complete bibliographic form.

1. a fantasy novel by any writer

____

____

____

2. a spy novel by Tom Clancy

____

____

____

3. science fiction novel by any writer

____

____

____

4. a historical novel by James Fenimore Cooper

____

____

____

5. a mystery by P. D. James

____

____

____

6. a realistic novel by Alice Walker

____

____

____

7. a realistic novel by John Steinbeck

____

____

LESSON 21 Find Your Way: The Dewey Decimal Way

WORDS TO KNOW

division
a general subject area

philosophy
the study that tries to understand knowledge and reality

psychology
the science of the mind; the study of why people think and act they way they do

religion
the worship of a higher being, such as God, and the beliefs about a higher being

politics
the science of guiding or controlling government

More Words to Know on page 66

Class Practice

How do you find books on American history or music? In 1876, Melvil Dewey came up with a way to divide all knowledge into ten different general subject areas. It is called the Dewey Decimal Classification System. (*Decimal* means based on ten.) Each subject area, or division, is given a range of numbers. All nonfiction books are organized by the Dewey system. Here are the general divisions and their range of numbers. You might not know what some of these subjects are. They are defined in *Words to Know* on this page and the next page.

000–099 **General Knowledge** (reference books, encyclopedias, dictionaries)
100–199 Philosophy & Psychology
200–299 Religion
300–399 **Social Sciences** (government, law, politics, education)
400–499 **Languages** (all the languages of the world)
500–599 **Natural Sciences** (mathematics, biology, earth sciences, chemistry, astronomy)
600–699 Technology (medicine, applied sciences, engineering, home economics)
700–799 **The Arts** (music, painting, architecture, sports, games)
800–899 **Literature** (stories, poems, novels, plays)
900–999 **History** (history, biography, genealogy, geography, travel)

Use this list to write the number range and subject for each of these topics.

1. musical instruments ______________________________

2. short stories ______________________________

3. football ______________________________

4. The Panama Canal ______________________________

5. Egyptians ______________________________

6. the space shuttle ______________________________

7. sharks ______________________________

8. Spanish ______________________________

9. U.S. presidential elections ______________________________

WORDS TO KNOW

biology
the study of living things, such as plants and animals

technology
the use of knowledge

home economics
the science and practice of homemaking

architecture
the science of designing buildings; also the style of a building

genealogy
the study of family histories or family trees

Group Practice

Write the number range and subject for each of these topics. Use the list of general divisions of the Dewey system on page 65 of this lesson. Watch out! Some of these are tricky!

1. piano building

____

2. children's books

____

3. history of checkers

____

4. Old English

____

5. ancient shipping routes

____

6. religions in the United States

____

7. odd state laws

____

8. plant life in a rain forest

____

9. a dictionary of slang

____

10. American folk music

____

11. old church buildings

____

12. life story of Thomas Edison

____

Here are the titles of five nonfiction books. Write the number range and subject for each. Use the list of general divisions of the Dewey system. These are really tricky!

13. A *History of the English Language*

____

14. *Images of the Civil War: The Paintings of Mort Kunstler*

____

15. *Mexico: A History in Art*

____

16. *Elvis Presley: King of Rock and Roll*

____

17. *A Religious History of America*

____

DID YOU KNOW?

Books on ghosts are classified in the Philosophy and Psychology (100–199) division of the Dewey Decimal Classification System.

On Your Own

Try out your new knowledge of the Dewey system. Go to the library. Find a book in each of the general divisions. Write the titles and the numbers of the books you find.

1. 000–099 General Knowledge

____

2. 100–199 Philosophy and Psychology

____

3. 200–299 Religion

____

4. 300–399 Social Sciences

____

5. 400–499 Languages

____

6. 500–599 Natural Sciences and Mathematics

____

7. 600–699 Technology

____

8. 700–799 The Arts

____

9. 800–899 Literature

____

10. 900–999 History

____

Use the general divisions of the Dewey system to answer these questions. Write the subject and number range in the blanks.

11. Your friend is studying his family tree. What is the study of a family tree called?

____

12. You want to know why your little brother acts the way he does. What kind of book should you read?

____

13. You like to draw buildings. What subject should you study?

____

14. In school, you learned how a gasoline engine works. You used this information to fix a broken lawn mower. What do you call using what you know?

____

LESSON 22 Find Your Way: Detail on Dewey

WORDS TO KNOW

subdivision
a smaller division; a more detailed subject

Class Practice

Melvil Dewey started with ten general divisions of knowledge. Then he divided those divisions into ten smaller divisions. These smaller divisions are called **subdivisions**. Here is an example. These are the subdivisions of the general division **700–799 The Arts**. Some topics are also listed.

700–799 The Arts

710 **Civic & Landscape Art** (design of public parks, other public areas, and flower gardens)
720 **Architecture** (the history of building design; design of public, religious, and school buildings; design of homes)
730 **Plastic Arts & Sculpture** (sculpture, carving, molding, modeling, metal art)
740 **Drawing, Decoration, & Minor Arts** (drawing, interior decoration, textile arts, glass, furniture)
750 **Painting & Paintings** (history of painting; techniques, equipment, color)
760 **Graphic Arts & Prints** (printing, engraving, etching)
770 **Photography & Photographs** (techniques, equipment, processes)
780 **Music** (singing, music, musical instruments)
790 **Sports & Recreation** (indoor and outdoor games and sports, games of chance, horse riding, fishing, hunting, shooting)

Here is a list of topics. What subdivisions do they fall under? Write the Dewey subdivision number for each topic.

1. how to use a camera ____________
2. sailing ____________
3. Greek buildings ____________
4. flower gardens ____________
5. origins of football ____________
6. designing an easy chair ____________
7. how to mix oil paints ____________
8. rock-and-roll ____________
9. glass blowing ____________

DID YOU KNOW?

Archeologists believe that early Egyptians played a game like modern bowling nearly 7,000 years ago.

Group Practice

History 900–999

910 Geography & Travel
920 Biography & Genealogy
930 History of Ancient World
940 General History of Europe
950 General History of Asia
960 General History of Africa
970 General History of North America
980 General History of South America
990 General History of Other Areas

Here is a list of topics. Write the Dewey subdivision number for each topic. Use the subdivisions of History 900–999.

1. the oceans of the world ____________

2. life story of George Washington ____________

3. first peoples of North America ____________

4. how ancient Greeks lived ____________

Natural Sciences 500–599

510 **Mathematics** (arithmetic, algebra, geometry)
520 **Astronomy** (the universe, planets, Earth in space)
530 **Physics** (how solids, liquids, and gases act; heat, electricity)
540 **Chemistry** (composition, structure, and properties of substances)
550 **Earth Sciences** (geology, weather and climate, water bodies)
560 **Paleontology** (fossils of things that once lived)
570 **Life Sciences** (human races, biology, evolution)
580 **Botany** (plants)
590 **Zoology** (worms, fish, reptiles, amphibians, birds, mammals)

Write the Dewey subdivision number for each topic. Use the subdivisions of Natural Sciences 500–599.

5. Earth's path around the sun ____________

6. life of a whale ____________

7. why $2 + 2 = 4$ ____________

8. what diamonds are made of ____________

9. why heat makes water boil ____________

On Your Own

Here are some subdivisions of different general divisions.

340 Law
370 Education
390 Customs, Manners, Folklore
610 Medicine
640 Homemaking & Family Living
720 Architecture
750 Painting & Paintings
770 Photography & Photographs
780 Music
790 Sports & Recreation
910 Geography & Travel
920 Biography & Genealogy

Use this list to write the number for each of these topics.

1. good manners __________
2. how to do a family tree __________
3. weather at the North Pole __________
4. life of Washington Carver __________
5. bodybuilding __________
6. cooking a dinner __________
7. famous churches in Europe __________
8. the rules of baseball __________
9. diseases __________
10. Irish folk songs __________
11. education in England __________
12. U.S. court system __________
13. marriage customs in Japan __________
14. famous painters __________

Use the list of subdivisions above. Write the number of the subdivision that might have a book to help you with each of these problems.

15. You have been invited to a fancy dinner party. You need to know which fork to use. __________
16. Someone told you that your school building is in the Colonial style. You don't know what that means. __________
17. A new cafe has opened in your neighborhood. It serves rarebit. You want to know what rarebit is before you order it. __________
18. You want to know what a movie director does. __________
19. You just met someone who is from Nepal. You don't know where Nepal is. __________
20. A new student in school plays cricket. You don't know what cricket is. __________

LESSON 23 Find Your Way: Dewey Know Our Decimals?

WORDS TO KNOW

specific
limited or narrow in size; particular

call number
the number given to a book to show its place on the library shelves

Class Practice

The Dewey system has ten main divisions. Each division has ten subdivisions. Each subdivision is divided into ten smaller subdivisions. The number range for the general division History is 900–999. The subdivision number for the history of North America is 970. The subdivision number for the history of the United States is 973. Each subdivision becomes more **specific**, or narrow. Numbers on the right side of the decimal point show the order of the book on the library shelf.

Many books will have the same Dewey number. So, below the number will be some letters. These are the first few letters of the writer's last name. For example, a book by Stephen Hawking might have the call number 530.1 Hawk. The number and letters together are called the **call number**. Here is the list of numbers in the 973 subdivision, history of the United States.

973.1 Early history to 1607
973.2 Colonial period, 1607–1775
973.3 period of revolution and confederation, 1775–1789
973.4 Constitutional period, 1789–1809
973.5 1809–1845
973.6 1845–1861
973.7 Civil War, Abraham Lincoln, 1861–1865
973.8 Reconstruction period, 1865–1901
973.9 1901–Present

Use this list to write the subdivision number for each of these topics.

1. writers of the Constitution ________

2. the Roaring Twenties ________

3. discovery of oil in Texas, 1901 ________

4. the first Americans ________

5. Jamestown settlement of 1607 ________

6. the first Thanksgiving ________

7. Paul Revere's ride ________

8. the Vietnam War ________

9. the War of 1812 ________

10. Lincoln's assassination ________

11. American Revolution battles ________

12. California Gold Rush of 1849 ________

13. first moon walk, 1969 ________

14. Oklahoma Land Rush, 1889 ________

DID YOU KNOW?

Leonardo da Vinci lived from 1452 to 1519. He drew his idea of a flying machine. He called it the ornithopter.

Group Practice

Take a trip to the library. Find a book on each of the following topics. Write the title and call number of each. Here is the list of general divisions to get you started.

000–099	**General Knowledge** (reference books, encyclopedias, dictionaries)
100–199	**Philosophy & Psychology**
200–299	**Religion**
300–399	**Social Sciences** (government, law, politics, education)
400–499	**Languages** (all the languages of the world)
500–599	**Natural Sciences** (mathematics, biology, earth sciences, chemistry, astronomy)
600–699	**Technology** (medicine, applied sciences, engineering, home economics)
700–799	**The Arts** (music, painting, architecture, sports, games)
800–899	**Literature** (stories, poems, novels, plays)
900–999	**History** (history, biography, genealogy, geography, travel)

Topic	Call Number	Title
1. the Internet	________	____________________
2. rain forests	________	____________________
3. human behavior	________	____________________
4. fairy tales	________	____________________
5. the solar system	________	____________________
6. dinosaurs	________	____________________
7. trains	________	____________________
8. rock-and-roll music	________	____________________
9. Siberia	________	____________________
10. myths	________	____________________
11. silent movies	________	____________________
12. a U.S. president	________	____________________

HELPFUL HINTS

You can find the name and location of a book's publisher on the first page, called the *title page*.

Look on the next page, called the *copyright page*, to find the copyright year.

Look back at Lesson 15 to see the bibliographic form for a book.

On Your Own

Find a book for each of these Dewey decimal numbers. Write the complete bibliographic information for each book.

Call Number	Bibliographic Entry
1. 027	______________________
2. 220.52	______________________
3. 372.4	______________________
4. 424.1	______________________
5. 523.1	______________________
6. 648	______________________
7. 796.58	______________________
8. 822.33	______________________
9. 938	______________________
10. 940.54	______________________

LESSON 24 Find Your Way: What Is a Library Catalog?

WORDS TO KNOW

library catalog
the records of a library's materials

author card
library catalog card with the writer's name first

title card
library catalog card with the title of the book first

subject card
library catalog card with the topic of the book first

Class Practice

The **library catalog** is a tool that helps you find what you are looking for in the library. It is where the library keeps the records of its materials. Your library's catalog might be an actual card file or an online catalog. In a card file, the records are listed on separate cards and filed in drawers. All catalog cards are filed alphabetically. Here is an example of a catalog card:

> Paul, Doris A.
>
> 940.54 The Navajo Code Talkers/Doris A. Paul/
> Paul New York: Putnam Press, c1998.
> 350 p., 24 cm.
> Index.
> 1. Codes—Navajo Language. 2. World War II—Secret Codes.
> 3. Navajo Language.

Each book in the library usually has at least three cards. These are the **author card**, the **title card**, and the **subject card**. The author card lists the author's name first, then the title of the book, and then other information. The title card lists the title of the book first. The subject card lists the subject or topic of the book first. Each card for a book has the same call number. Here is a subject card for a book. Use it to answer the questions.

> MUSIC—AMERICAN
>
> 781.6 Wood, Elijah
> Wood Purely American Music: From Folk to Jazz/ Elijah Wood/New York: Putnam Press, c2000.
> 256 p., col. ill., 24 cm.
> Index.
> 1. Folk music. 2. Country-western music.
> 3. Jazz

1. What is the title of the book?

____

2. What is the call number? ________________

3. How many pages is the book? ________________

4. What is the author's last name? ________________

5. What subject is this card filed under?

____

Group Practice

Here are three sample catalog cards. Use the first card to answer Questions 1–5. Use the second card to answer Questions 6–10. Use the third card to answer Questions 11–15.

PSYCHOLOGY—SELF-HELP

158 Russell-McCloud, Patricia
Russ A Is for Attitude: An Alphabet for Living/ Patricia Russell-McCloud/New York: Guilford Press, c1999.
305p., 28 cm.
Index.
1. Psychology—Self-Help. 2. Self-Help

1. Is this an author, title, or subject card? ____________

2. What is the author's full name?

____

3. How many pages does the book have?____________

4. What is the title of the book?

____

5. What year was the book published?____________

A History of the English Language

420.9 Baugh, Albert C., Thomas Cable
Bau A History of the English Language/ Albert C. Baugh and Thomas Cable/ Englewood Cliffs, NJ: Prentice-Hall, c1978.
438 p., 24 cm.
Index and Bibliography.
1. English Language—History

6. Is this an author, title, or subject card? ____________

7. What are the last names of the two authors?

____

8. What subject would you find this book under?

____

9. What is the call number of the book? ____________

10. Who is the publisher?

____

Tuchman, Barbara W.

973.35 The First Salute: A View of the
Tuch American Revolution
Barbara W. Tuchman/New York: Alfred A. Knopf, c1988.
347 p., 24 cm.
Index and Bibliography.
1. United States—History—Revolution, 1775–1783—Naval operations. 2. United States—History—Revolution, 1775–1783—Campaigns.

11. Is this an author, title, or subject card? ____________

12. What is the title of the book?

____

13. Who is the author of this book?

____

14. What is the call number of this book?____________

15. How many pages does the book have?____________

On Your Own

Here are two sample catalog cards. Use the first card to answer Questions 1–5. Use the second card to answer Questions 6–10.

UNITED STATES—CHURCH HISTORY

291.0973 Gaustad, Edwin Scott
Gaus A Religious History of America/
Edwin Scott Gaustad/San Francisco:
Harper SanFrancisco, c1966.
391p., 24 cm., photographs
Includes Bibliographies and Index.
1. United States—Church History.

1. Is this an author, title, or subject card? ______

2. What is the author's full name?

______

3. What subject would you find this book under?

______

4. What is the title of the book?

______

5. What is the call number of this book? ______

Hawking, Stephen W.

530.1 Black Holes and Baby Universes
Hawk and Other Essays
Stephen Hawking/New York: Bantam Books,
c1993.
182 p.
Index.
1. Hawking, Stephen W. 2. Cosmology.
3. Science—Philosophy. 4. Physicists—
Great Britain—Biography

6. Is this an author, title, or subject card? ______

7. What is the title of this book?

______

8. What two subjects would you find this book under?

______

9. What is the call number of the book? ______

10. Who is the publisher?

______

Find three books on a topic that interests you. List that topic. For each book, write the call number and the full bibliographic entry.

Subject: ______

11. Book 1: ______

______

12. Book 2: ______

______

13. Book 3: ______

______

LESSON 25 Find Your Way: What Is an Online Catalog?

Class Practice

Your school library or public library might have an online catalog. An online catalog is a listing of the library's books on a computer system. You can find the same information in an online catalog as you can find in library catalog cards:

the call number
the author's name
the title of the book
the name and location of the publisher
the year the book was published
the different subjects, or topics, related to the book

When you search for a book by the author's name, type the author's last name first. You can also search for a book by the title. Do not type the first word of the title if it is *A*, *An*, or *The*. These words are so common that the computer ignores them. You can also find books by subject. To find a book by subject, you type in key words.

Here is a list of authors, titles, and subjects. Write the words that you would type to find books in the online library catalog.

1. *A Wrinkle in Time* (a book) ______________________
2. the effects of acid rain on plant life ______________________
3. Mark Twain (a writer) ______________________
4. the life of actor Harrison Ford ______________________
5. *The Color Purple* (a book) ______________________
6. how special effects are done in movies ______________________
7. Herman Melville (a writer) ______________________
8. what you need to know to sky dive ______________________
9. Isaac Asimov (a writer) ______________________
10. *The Yearling* (a book) ______________________
11. what makes lava come from a volcano ______________________
12. J. K. Rowling (a writer) ______________________
13. people who have climbed Mount Everest ______________________
14. *The Good Earth* (a book) ______________________

DID YOU KNOW?

The largest public library in the United States is the New York Public Library. It has over 11 million books.

Group Practice

Use your library's online catalog or card catalog to find the answers to these questions. Be sure to write the call number and a complete bibliographic entry for each book.

1. a biography of Theodore Roosevelt, 26th president of the United States

2. a book by Judy Bloom

3. a book about hurricanes

4. What other subjects are listed on the entry for the book about hurricanes?

5. a book about the history of movie make-up

6. a book by Theodore Roosevelt

7. a book by Jack London

DID YOU KNOW?

The largest university library in the United States is the Harvard University Library. It has over 13 million books.

On Your Own

Use your library's online catalog or card catalog to find the answers to these questions. Be sure to write the call number and a complete bibliographic entry for each book.

1. a book about national parks in the United States

   ____

   ____

   ____

2. What other subjects are listed on the entry for the book about national parks?

   ____

   ____

   ____

3. a book on one of the other subjects listed with the book on national parks

   ____

   ____

   ____

the way American women dressed in the late 1800s

the art of glass blowing

mammals of North America

the settlement of the American West

car racing

Pick one of the subjects in the box. Find three books by three different authors on that subject. Be sure to write the call number and a complete bibliographic entry for each book.

4. ______________________________

   ____

   ____

   ____

5. ______________________________

   ____

   ____

   ____

6. ______________________________

   ____

   ____

   ____

LESSON 26 Find Your Way: Caught in the Web

WORDS TO KNOW

Internet
a network of computers around the world

Web site
a page on the Internet

directory
a collection of Web sites grouped by categories

category
a broad subject or topic

search box
a space on a Web site to type in key words about a topic

Class Practice

The **Internet** is a huge network that connects computers around the world. Through the Internet, you can connect to the World Wide Web. The Web is a collection of millions of Web sites. A **Web site** is a page on the Internet. The Web is a great way to do research, but how do you begin?

One way to search for information is with a directory. A **directory** is a collection of Web sites that are grouped into categories. A **category** is a broad subject or topic. Under each category is a list of smaller categories. A directory also has a search box. The **search box** is where you type in words about the information you need. When you search for information in a directory, only those Web sites in that directory are searched. Here is a sample directory called TellMeMore!

Use the TellMeMore! directory page to answer these questions.

1. Which major category would you click to find information on kangaroos?

____

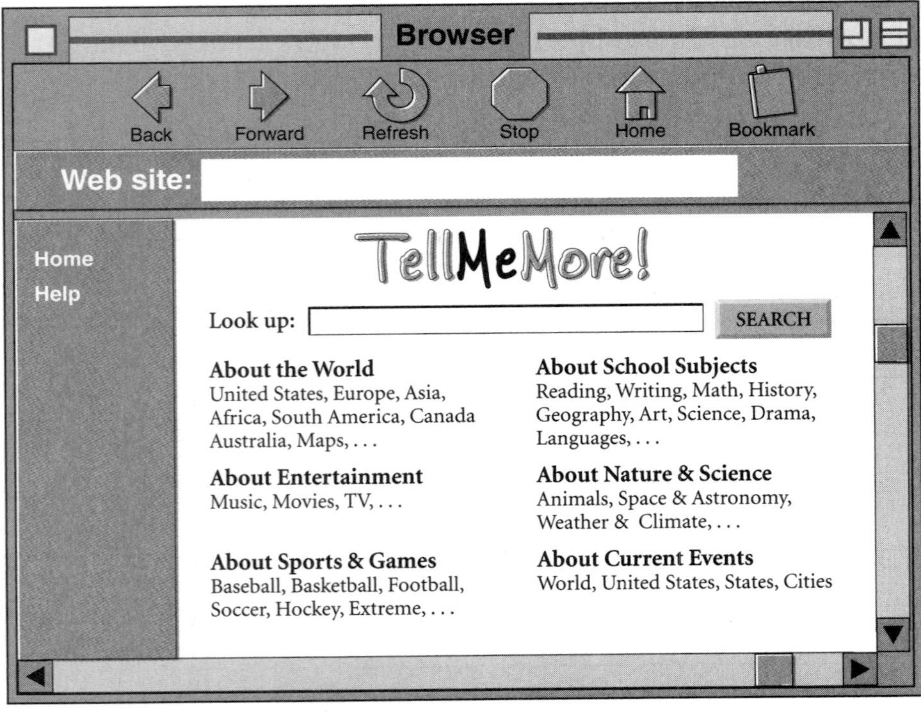

2. Which major category would you click to find information on Russia?

____

____

3. Which major category might give you help with your homework?

____

____

Group Practice

Look at the TellMeMore! directory page again. Under the category *About Nature & Science* is a smaller category *Space & Astronomy*. If you click that smaller category, you will see this page. This page lists topics and Web sites about space and astronomy. Beside each category is a number in parentheses, for example, *Black Holes* (6). That is the number of Web sites about black holes. If you click that topic, you will see the list of six Web sites.

Use this page to answer Questions 1–3.

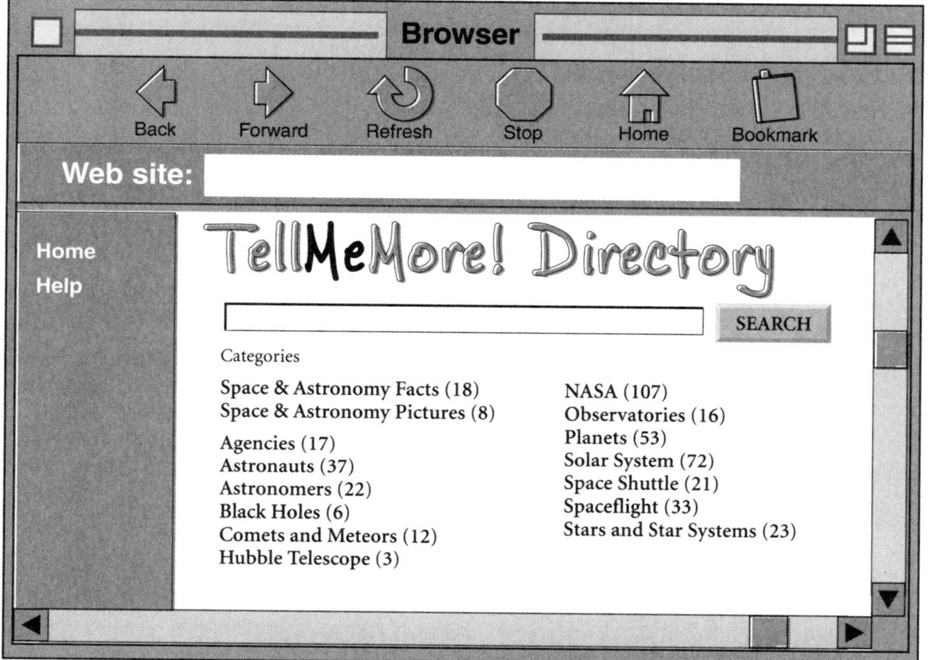

1. How many Web sites are listed for *Solar System*?

____

2. Which topic would you click to find information about the planet Mars?

____

3. Which topic would you click to find information about the effects of flying in space?

____

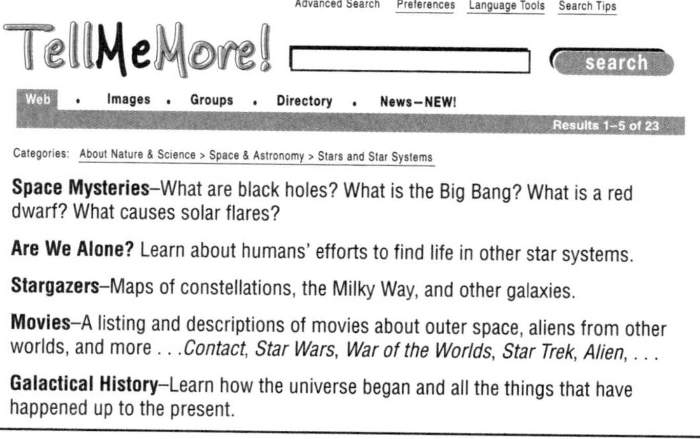

If you click the category *Stars and Star Systems*, here are some of the Web sites you would see.

Use these Web sites to answer Questions 4–6.

4. Which Web site would tell you how the universe started?

____

5. Which Web site would have maps of star systems?

____

6. Which Web site is about beings from other worlds?

____

DID YOU KNOW?

A German scientist named Wilhelm Schickard invented the first machine used for computing. He invented it in 1623!

On Your Own

Now it's time for you to actually do some searching on a computer! The answers to these questions can be found on a Web site owned by Seaworld. The Web address is **http://www.seaworld.org/infobook.html**.

Find the Web site. Click on the category Animal Bytes**. When that directory page appears, click on the smaller category** Warthog**. Answer these questions.**

1. What is the scientific name for a warthog?

 ____

2. Why is this animal called a warthog?

 ____

 ____

3. What is a group of warthogs called? ______________________________

4. How long does a warthog usually live?

 ____

5. How do warthogs go into their burrows?

 ____

 ____

HELPFUL HINT

Every Web site on the Internet has an address. This address is called a URL. URL stands for Uniform Resource Locator. For example, the address for the National Aeronautics & Space Administration (NASA) is **http://www.nasa.gov.**

The answers to these questions can be found at the Web site owned by the U.S. Field Hockey Association: http://www.usfieldhockey.com. Click on International Games**, then on** Olympic Symbols **in the right-hand column.**

6. What are the colors of the Olympic rings?

 ____

7. What do the rings stand for?

 ____

8. Who wrote the words of the Olympic Creed?

 ____

9. When was the first Olympic Oath?

 ____

10. What was the site of the first Olympic Games?

 ____

11. What does the Olympic Motto "Citius, Altius, Fortius" mean?

 ____

LESSON 27 Find Your Way: Start Your Engines!

WORDS TO KNOW

search engine
a Web page used to search the entire Internet for information

Class Practice

You have learned to use directory pages and categories to find information on the Internet. **Search engines** are similar to directories because they are also a way to find information on the Internet. Search engine Web pages look like directory Web pages and have addresses (URLs). A search engine is different from a directory because it searches the entire Internet for Web sites that might have information on your topic.

With some search engines, you find information in the same way you find information on a directory page. You click on categories. Here is a sample search engine Web page that has categories for searching.

Use the KnowItAll Web page to answer these questions.

1. Which major category would lead to information about spooky happenings? ______________________

2. Which major category and minor category would lead to information about your favorite actor or actress?

____

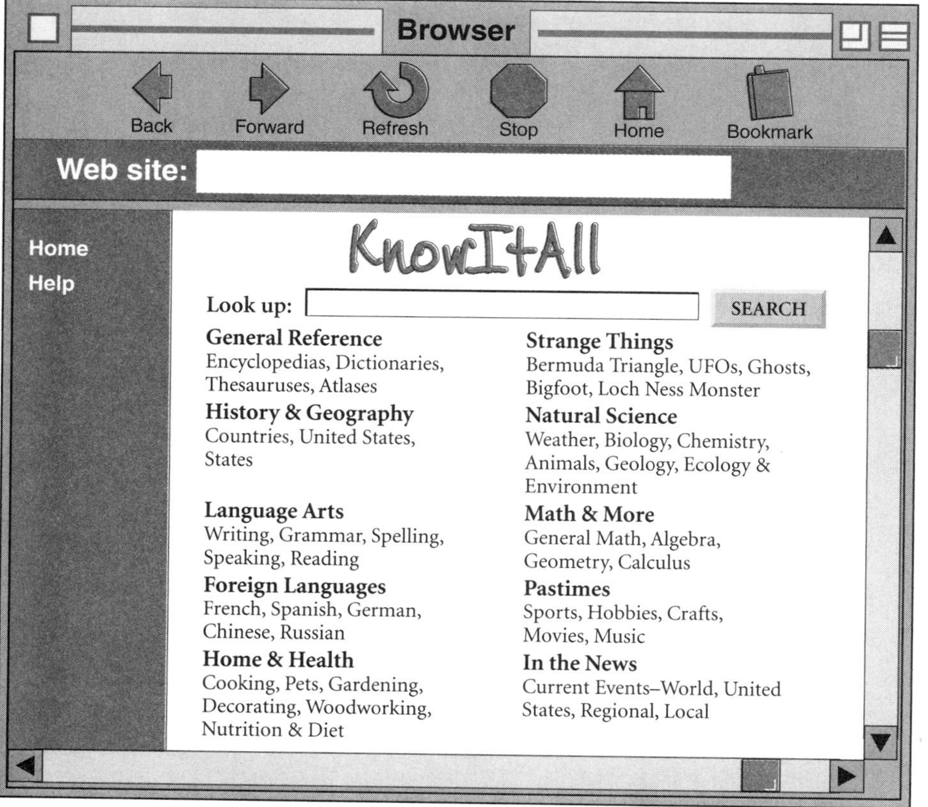

3. Which major category and minor category would lead to information about model airplanes?

____

____

4. Which major category and minor category would lead to the latest information on the U.S. Congress?

____

____

5. Which major category and minor category would lead to information on synonyms?

____

____

Group Practice

If you click the minor category *Animals* under *Natural Science* on the KnowItAll Web page, you will see this page. This page lists many topics. It lists types of animals, such as reptiles, and also specific animals.

Use this page to answer these questions.

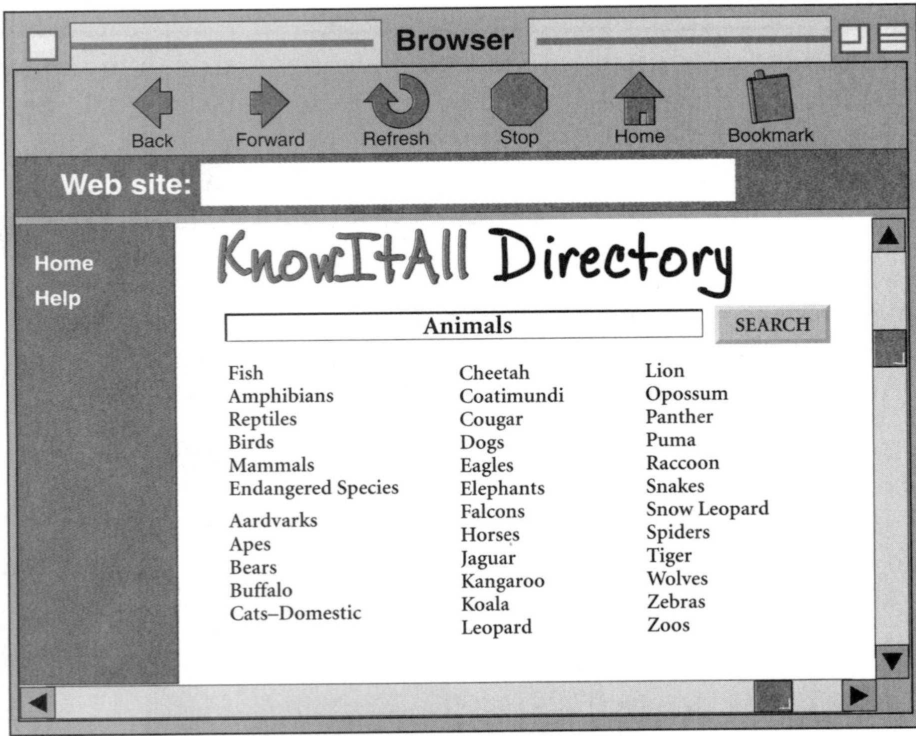

1. Which topic would have information about parrots?

____

2. Which topic would have information about sharks?

____

3. Which topic would tell you about animals that might disappear forever?

____

____

4. Which topic would have information about the San Diego Zoo?

____

If you click the topic *Wolves* on this page, you will see this page of listed Web sites.

Use this page to answer these questions.

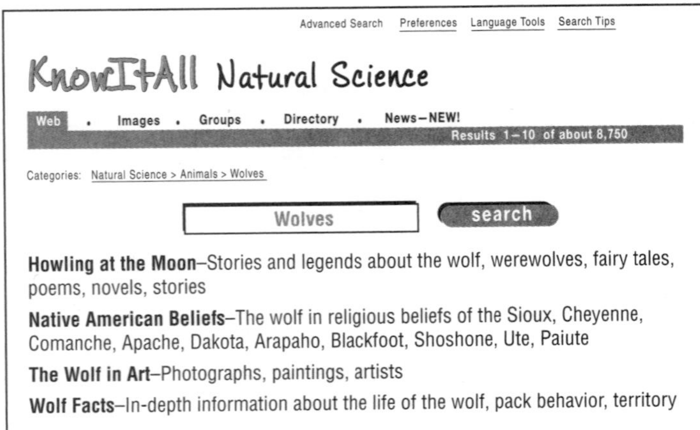

5. Which Web site has pictures of wolves?

____

6. Which Web site has poems about the wolf?

____

7. Which Web site tells about the wolf in religious beliefs?

____

8. Which Web site would tell you where wolves live?

____

On Your Own

Follow these steps to find the answers to these questions. Find the search engine KidsClick! at http://sunsite.berkeley.edu/KidsClick! Under the major category Science & Math, click on the minor category Animals. When that page appears, click on the topic Puffins. Click on the Web site Scientific Family Animal Bytes: Puffins.

1. What is the Order name for puffins? ______________________
2. How fast can a puffin fly? ______________________
3. Puffins can dive deeper than ______________________ to catch fish.
4. What are a puffin's natural predators? ______________________
5. How many eggs does a female puffin lay each year? ______________

Now, it's your turn. Using the same search engine, KidsClick!, pick an animal that interests you. Answer these questions.

6. Which animal did you choose? ______________________
7. Which Web site did you use for your information? ______________
8. What is the Species name of this animal? ______________________

   ____

9. What does this animal eat? ______________________
10. Where does this animal live in the wild? List the country or continent.

    ____

DID YOU KNOW?

Every state in the United States has had a tornado.

To answer these questions, find the Web site NSSL Tornado Information. The NSSL Internet address is: http://www.nssl.noaa .gov/ edu/tornado.

11. On which continents have tornadoes occurred?

    ____

12. What is the fastest a tornado has moved? ______________________
13. What does TOTO stand for? ______________________
14. What movie was based on actual work by the NSSL?

    ____

15. What does NSSL stand for? (This is hard! Can you find the answer?)

    ____

LESSON 28 Find Your Way: What's the Word?

WORDS TO KNOW

key words
the most important words that identify a topic

Class Practice

You know how to use directory pages and search engines with categories to find information on the Internet. Some search engines do not have categories to click on. These search engines require questions or key words to search for information. Key words are the most important words that identify your topic. Here are some search engines that require you to use key words:

Kid's Search Tools	**http://www.rcls.org/ksearch.htm**
Ask Jeeves	**http://www.ask.com**
Teoma	**http://www.teoma.com**

When you click on categories on a directory page or search engine page, you are really choosing key words to narrow your search. But the people who designed the page picked the key words for you. When you use the search box on a Web page, you choose and type in your own key words. Remember that the Internet has millions of Web sites and millions and millions of pages of information. If you know how to choose good key words, you will not have to read those millions of pages to find the information you need! The right key words will narrow your search. Here are things to remember when you use key words:

- **Be sure to spell the words correctly.** A search engine searches for what you type. If you type **alligaters** the search engine will not find Web sites about **alligators**.
- **Be specific.** If you want information on English sports cars, type **English sports cars,** not **cars.**
- **Follow the rules.** Most directory pages and search engines have rules on how to use key words. If you are searching for baseball rules, sometimes you just type the words **baseball rules**. Sometimes you might have to put quotation marks around the words, **"baseball rules."** Sometimes you might have to connect the words with a dash: **baseball-rules**.

DID YOU KNOW?

Of the 50 states in the United States, the names of 27 states come from American Indian languages.

Group Practice

Which key words would you use for these searches?

1. You just made a new friend who is from China. You want to know something about the culture of China.

   ____

2. You want to learn about the giant snakes that live in the Amazon River of South America.

   ____

3. You have heard good things and bad things about chocolate. You want the real story.

   ____

4. You just saw a movie with unicorns. You want to know more about unicorns and other mythical creatures.

   ____

5. The last time you played tag football, there was an argument about the rules. You want to know the real rules.

   ____

Now try this experiment. Use one of the search engines listed on the first page of this lesson or one that you like. Keep in mind that you want to find information on the wild lions that live in Africa.

6. In the search box, type this word: **lions**
   How many Web pages did this search find?______________
7. This time, in the search box, type these words: **wild lions in Africa**
   How many Web pages did this search find?______________
8. This time, in the search box, type these words: **African lion**
   How many Web pages did this search find?______________
9. From the first ten Web sites, list three that do not seem to be on target.

   ____

   ____

   ____

10. Now, in the search box, type these words: **African-lion**
    How many Web pages did this search find?______________
11. Are the first 10 Web sites about African lions? ______________

On Your Own

Try your own search on a topic that interests you. Use one of these search engines or one you like.

Kid's Search Tools	**http://www.rcls.org/ksearch.htm**
Ask Jeeves	**http://www.ask.com**
Teoma	**http://www.teoma.com**

1. What is your topic?

____

2. Which search engine did you use?

____

3. What key words did you use the first time?

____

4. How many Web sites did this search result in?

____

5. What key words did you use the second time?

____

6. How many Web sites did this search result in?

____

7. What key words did you use last?

____

8. How many Web sites did this search result in?

____

9. List five Web sites that you think will give you the information you need. List them in the order, with the best one first. Give the name and the Internet address for each one.

____

____

____

____

____

LESSON 29 Find Your Way: A Few More Tips

WORDS TO KNOW

extension
the part of an Internet address that identifies the type of organization that owns the site

Class Practice

You know how to find information on the Internet. Now you need to know which information is correct or truthful. One way to know that information is good is by the Internet address, or URL. One part of an Internet address is called the **extension**. The extension usually comes at the end of the address. The extension can tell you what type of organization is providing the information. Here are the most common extensions and examples:

.org	organizations that help people or causes	**http://www.seaworld.org**
.gov	government agencies and departments	**http://www.nasa.gov**
.edu	schools, colleges, and universities	**http://www.stanford.edu**
.com	businesses and individuals	**http://www.agsnet.com**

Another thing to know when you use the Internet is how to cite your source. Here is a basic form for citing an Internet source:

> Author's name (if given). "Title of article." *Name of Web site.* Date article was posted. <Web address>. Date article was retrieved.

The article from the NOAA (National Oceanic and Atmospheric Administration) site is like an article from a newspaper. The bibliography entry looks like one for a newspaper, but it includes the Internet address. If you use a direct quotation, put quotation marks around the words. A direct quotation is treated the same way you treat a quotation from a written source but without a page number.

You also need to know how to print the information. You can print the whole article or just part of it.

Use these steps to print the whole article:

1. Click on the File menu.
2. Click on Print.
3. When the Print dialog box appears, click on OK.

Use these steps to print just part of an article:

1. Select the information with the cursor.
2. Click on the File menu.
3. Click on Print.
4. When the Print dialog box appears, click on Selection.
5. Click on OK.

HELPFUL HINTS

Guidelines for Picking Web Sites

The information is well-organized and easy to find.

There are clear instructions for using special features.

The content is well written, with correct spelling and grammar.

There is not too much advertising.

The site does not seem to have any bad messages.

The site does not ask for personal information before you can use it. If it does, leave the site immediately.

Group Practice

For each question, place a check mark in front of your answer.

1. Which Web site might be the best source of information on the weather in North America?
   ___ **http://www.NOAA.gov** Web site of the National Oceanic and Atmospheric Administration
   ___ **http://www.ruinedvacation.com** Personal pictures of a rained-out trip to California
   ___ **http://twister!.com** Pictures of a tornado taken by a local reporter in Oklahoma

2. Which Web site might be the best source of information on how to care for a kitten?
   ___ **http://www.petpictures.com** Pictures of someone's pet cat
   ___ **http://www.dogsforsale.com** Advertisement by someone who raises Irish setters
   ___ **http://vet.cornell.edu/Public/FHC/newcat.html** Web site of Cornell University School of Veterinary Medicine

3. Which Web site might be the best source of information on a current news story?
   ___ **http://www.pastandpresent.com** Web site owned by a history student
   ___ **http://www.cnn.com** Web site of CNN News
   ___ **http://www.wantads.com** Online want ads by a local newspaper

Write these sources in correct bibliographic form.

4. An article called "Bargains Galore at Stores" on the *CNN Money* Web site, dated December 26, 2002. Internet address: http://money.cnn.com/2002/12/26/news/economy/post_holiday.ap/index.htm, accessed today.

   ____

   ____

   ____

5. An article called "States' Rights" from *Microsoft Encarta Online Encyclopedia 2002*. Copyright date 1993–2002 by Microsoft Corporation Internet address is http://encarta.msn.com, accessed today.

   ____

   ____

   ____

On Your Own

Answer these questions about Web sites. Write true or false in the blank.

1. A Web site that has a lot of advertisements and is trying to sell you something is a good site for research. ____________
2. Web sites by the U.S. government have addresses that end in .gov. ____________
3. A really good Web site asks for personal information before you can use it. ____________
4. A Web site that ends in .edu is probably a good site for research. ____________
5. You do not have to include Internet sources in your bibliography. ____________
6. A Web site address that ends in .com is probably owned by a business or individual. ____________
7. Find an article from an online news source about a topic that interests you. The source might be a national television network or your local newspaper or television station. Print one paragraph from that article. Write the source in correct bibliographic form.

____

____

____

Pick an animal that interests you. Find three different sources of information about that animal on the Internet. Write the sources in correct bibliographic form.

8. ____

____

____

9. ____

____

____

10. ____

____

____

LESSON 30 Putting It All Together

Class Practice

You have learned quite a lot from these lessons about doing research. Now is your chance to show what you have learned. In this last lesson, you will find several sources of information about a particular topic. Then you will write a summary for each source and write the source in correct bibliographic form. When you have done all of this, you will be well on your way to writing a research paper!

Remember to use the correct bibliographic form for your sources. Refer to Lessons 15 and 29 for examples.

Here are some Web sites, listed by subject, that might help you in your research.

General

http://www.rcls.org/ksearch.htm
http://www.ipl.org
http://www.exploratorium.edu/explore
http://thorplus.lib.purdue.edu/eresources/readyref

Science and Technology

http://www.nasa.gov
http://www.noaa.gov
http://www.seaworld.org
http://www.nssl.noaa.gov
http://info.er.usgs.gov
http://www.learner.org/exhibits

Social Studies

http://www.odci.gov/cia/publications/factbook
http://www.ipl.org/ref/POTUS
http://www.census.gov/main/www/subjects.html
http://marvel.loc.gov/homepage/lchp.html

News and Current Events

http://www.cnn.com
http://news.bbc.co.uk

Words

http://www.wordsmyth.net
http://www.m-w.com

List Web sites that you have used and liked:

______________________ ______________________

______________________ ______________________

______________________ ______________________

______________________ ______________________

______________________ ______________________

______________________ ______________________

Group Practice

Pick a topic to research. Make sure your topic is narrow enough to write about in five pages. For example, you might be interested in weather. Think about all the topics that *weather* can include: rain, clouds, tornados, hurricanes, snow, El Niño, weather patterns in each part of the world, and so on! You could not write about all those things in five pages. Perhaps you are interested in history. Think of all the history in the world! You could not write about all the history in the world in only five pages! So, you need to narrow your topic. The members of your group can help.

RESEARCH TOPIC

____

____

____

____

____

Write your general topic idea here and discuss it with your group. List the ideas for narrow topics that you come up with. When you decide on the specific topic that you want to research, write it in the green box at the left.

General Topic Idea: ______________________

Specific Topics: ______________________

____

____

____

On Your Own

Find information on your topic from five different sources, including:

a magazine article
an article from a reference book
an article, either from a newspaper or an online news Web site
an article from a general Web site
an article from a specific Web site

For each source, write the correct bibliographic form and a summary of the information.

Magazine Article

Bibliographic Entry: ______________________

____

Summary: ______________________

____

____

____

____

Reference Book Article

Bibliographic Entry: ______________________________

____

Summary: ______________________________

____

____

____

____

News Article

Bibliographic Entry: ______________________________

____

Summary: ______________________________

____

____

____

____

General Web Site Article

Bibliographic Entry: ______________________________

____

Summary: ______________________________

____

____

____

____

Special Web Site Article

Bibliographic Entry: ______________________________

____

Summary: ______________________________

____

____

____

____

GLOSSARY

abbreviation (ə brē vē ā´ shən) a short form of a word (p. 59)

alphabetical order (al fə bet´ ə kəl ôr´ dər) the order of the letters of the alphabet, from A to Z (p. 5)

antonym (an´ tə nim) a word that means the opposite of another word (p. 23)

architecture (är´ kə tek chər) the science of designing buildings; also the style of a building (p. 65)

author card (ȯ´ thər kärd) library catalog card with the writer's name first (p. 74)

autobiography (ȯ tə bī og´ rə fē) a book written by a person about his or her own life (p. 56)

banner (ban´ ər) the name of a newspaper (p. 35)

bibliography (bib lē og´ rə fē) a list of sources used in a research paper (p. 47)

biography (bī og´ rə fē) a book written about an actual person's life (p. 56)

biology (bī ol´ ə jē) the study of living things, such as plants and animals (p. 65)

call number (kȯl num´ ber) the number given to a book to show its place on the library shelves (p. 71)

caption (kap´ shən) the title or explanation of a photograph, illustration, or map (p. 32)

category (kat´ e gôr ē) a broad subject or topic (p. 80)

cite (sīt) to name a source (p. 44)

classified advertisements (klas´ ə fīd ad vər tīz´ mentz) a section of a newspaper that lists jobs and things for sale (p. 35)

context (kon´ tekst) words surrounding a word in a sentence that can shed light on its meaning (p. 17)

cue (kyü) a signal or a hint (p. 8)

daily (dā´ lē) every day (p. 35)

definition (def ə nish´ ən) the meaning of a word (p. 11)

directory (də rek´ tər ē) a collection of Web sites grouped by categories (p. 80)

division (də vizh´ ən) a general subject area (p. 65)

editorial (ed ə tôr´ ē əl) an article in a newspaper or magazine giving the writer's views (p. 35)

entry (en´ trē) a single source listed in a bibliography (p. 47)

extension (ek sten´ shən) the part of an Internet address that identifies the type of organization that owns the site (p. 89)

fact (fakt) something that can be proved (p. 38)

factual (fak´ chü əl) based on facts (p. 38)

fantasy (fan´ tə sē) a story, such as a fairy tale, set in a world that is not real and with characters that are unreal (p. 62)

fiction (fik´ shən) a story drawn from the writer's imagination (p. 62)

fiction book (fik´ shən bu̇k) a book that tells a story; a *novel* (p. 56)

genealogy (jē nē al´ a jē) the study of family histories or family trees (p. 65)

genre (zhän´ rə) kind of book or short story (p. 62)

guide words (gīd wėrdz) two words at the top of a page in a dictionary (p. 11)

headline (hed´ līn) the guide words in a reference book (p. 32)

historical fiction (hi stôr´ ə kəl fik´ shən) a story set in an actual time and place with make believe characters (p. 62)

home economics (hōm ē kə nom´ iks) the science and practice of homemaking (p. 65)

idiom (id´ ē əm) a phrase that does not mean what its individual words mean (p. 26)

illustration (ilə strā´ shən) example of something in the form of a picture; a drawing (p. 32)

index (in´ deks) a list of topics and page numbers in a book (p. 29)

Internet (in´ tər net) a network of computers around the world (p. 80)

issue (ish´ ü) a single printing of a magazine (p. 41)

issue number (ish´ ü num´ bər) a number given to a single printing of a magazine (p. 41)

journal (jėr´ nl) a magazine (p. 41)

key words (kē wėrdz) the most important words that identify a topic (p. 86)

lexicon (lek´ sə kən) a dictionary (p. 8)

library catalog (lī´ brer´ ē kat´ e log) the records of a library's materials (p. 74)

main idea (mān ī dē´ ə) a statement of what an article is about (p. 50)

multimedia (mul ti mē´ dē ə) material other than printed materials, such as CD ROMs and videocassettes (p. 56)

mystery (mis´ tər ē) a story that sets up a problem to be solved, such as a crime or a strange event; also called a *whodunit* (p. 62)

nonfiction book (non fik´ shən bu̇k) a book about things that actually happened (p. 56)

novel (nov´ əl) a fiction book (p. 62)

opinion (ə pin´ yən) someone's belief or view (p. 38)

periodical (pir ē od´ ə kəl) something printed at regular times, such as newspapers and magazines (p. 41)

periodical index (pir ē od´ ə kəl in´ deks) a publication that lists magazine articles by subject and title (p. 59)

philosophy (fə los´ ə fē) the study that tries to understand knowledge and reality (p. 65)

photograph (fō tə graf) a picture taken with a camera (p. 32)

phrase (frāz) a group of words (p. 26)

plagiarism (plā´ jə riz əm) copying or using another's work and passing it off as your own (p. 44)

politics (pol´ ə tiks) the science of guiding or controlling government (p. 65)

psychology (sī kol´ ə jē) the science of the mind; study of why people think and act the way they do (p. 65)

quarterly (kwôr´ tər lē) printed four times a year (p. 41)

quotation marks (kwō tā´ shən märks) marks that surround words taken directly from a source (p. 47)

realistic fiction (rē ə lis´ tik fik´ shen) a story set in an actual time and place with make believe characters (p. 62)

reference book (ref´ ər əns bu̇k) a book of facts and information about one or more topics (p. 29)

religion (ri lij´ ən) worship of a higher being, such as God, and the beliefs about a higher being (p. 65)

research (ri sėrch) the careful collection of information about a topic (p. 29)

running head (run´ ing hed) name, day, date, and page number at the top of each page of a newspaper (p. 35)

scan (skan) to read quickly to find out what something is generally about (p. 50)

science fiction (sī´ əns fik´ shən) story set in the future, on another planet, or in an imaginary time or place (p. 62)

search box (sėrch boks) a space on a Web site to type in key words about a topic (p. 80)

search engine (sėrch en´ jən) a Web page used to search the entire Internet for information (p. 83)

section (sek´ shən) a part, such as part of a newspaper (p. 35)

skim (skim) to look quickly for a particular piece of information (p. 50)

slang (slang) usage that is not widely accepted or known (p. 14)

society (sə sī´ ə tē) people in a community (p. 35)

source (sôrs) the work where information was found (p. 44)

specific (spi sif´ ik) limited or narrow in size; particular (p. 71)

standard (stan´ dərd) widely accepted usage (p. 14)

subdivision (sub də vizh´ ən) a smaller division; a more detailed subject (p. 68)

subhead (sub´ hed) a smaller heading used for a paragraph (p. 32)

subject card (sub´ jikt kärd) library catalog card with the topic of the book first (p. 74)

summary (sum´ ər ē) the point about the main idea that the writer is trying to make (p. 50)

synonym (sin´ ə nim) a word that has the same or nearly the same meaning as another word (p. 20)

technology (tek nol´ ə jē) use of knowledge (p. 65)

thesaurus (thi sôr´ əs) a book of synonyms (p. 20)

title card (tīt´ l kärd) library catalog card with the title of the book first (p. 74)

topic (top´ ik) a subject; what a research paper is about (p. 29)

usage (yü sij) the ways a word is used (p. 14)

volume number (vol´ yəm num´ bər) a number given to a set of magazines (p. 41)

want ads (wänt ads) another name for classified advertisements (p. 35)

Web site (web sīt) a page on the Internet (p. 80)

weekly (wēk´ lē) every week (p. 35)